HOW TO START A CAREER IN INFORMATION TECHNOLOGY

BY IAN K. FISHER

Published by:
Ian K. Fisher
P.O. box 10562
Oakland, California 94610
ikfisher@onebox.com
(866)877-9791 phone/fax

To order see page 135.

1st printing
ISBN print edition   0-9760052-0-4
ISBN PDF edition   0-9760052-1-2
ISBN cassette edition 0-9760052-2-0

DEDICATION

This book is dedicated to our daughter Alicia Lorena Fisher, the light of my life! Thank you for being you. September 2004.

ACKNOWLEDGEMENTS

This book was shaped by the ideas and opinions of many. This book would not have been possible without the help of the esteemed professionals listed below. Before I acknowledge them let me first thank my wife Maria Lorena who took care of the baby for two years while I worked on the book. (And who brought me countless snacks late at night.) Thank you to my mother and father, Myrtha Ofelia Chabrán-Acevedo and Sethard Fisher who have given me everything, and were the first to read the book. All gave of their time and expertise, in an effort to help make this book a reality. All the shortcomings of the book are my own, and should not reflect on those acknowledged here.

A special thank you to my students, who are the reason for this book, and who have helped me realize there was a need for it. To Mitsu Fisher; Cynthia Cravens of Jewish Vocational Services in San Francisco; Merble Reagon, Executive Director of the Women's Center, New York City; Dennis Green, Director of Information Technology Programs, Columbia University, New York City; Dr. Richard Vigilante, Executive Director, Jesuit Distance Education Network, New York, NY; M. Sumyyah Bilal, Executive Director, EUREKA; Roger Moncarz of U.S. Department of Labor, Bureau of Labor Statistics, Washington, D.C.; Karin Nelson of San Francisco City College; Mark Butler of BayTEC, Oakland, California; Dr. Lois Blades-Rosado, State

University of New York-Brooklyn Educational
Opportunity Center; Lenny Bailes; Philip Laird;
Kathleen Creighton of Pratt Institute-Career Services,
Brooklyn, NY; and Igor Ovchinikov, Glide
Foundation, San Francisco, CA.

DISCLAIMER

This book is designed to provide information on how to start a career in information technology. It is sold with the understanding that the publisher and author are not engaged in rendering legal, accounting, or other professional services.

It is not the purpose of this book to reprint all the information that is otherwise available to career seekers, but instead to complement, amplify, and supplement other texts. You are urged to read all the available material, learn as much as possible, and tailor the information to your individual needs. A career in IT is not a get-rich-quick scheme. Anyone who decides to pursue an IT career must expect to invest a lot of time and effort into it.

Every effort has been made to make this book as complete and as accurate as possible. However, there *may be mistakes,* both typographical and in content. Therefore, this book should be used only as a general guide and not as the ultimate source. Furthermore, this book contains information on IT careers that is current only up to the printing date.

The author and publisher shall have neither liability nor responsibility to any person or entity with respect to any loss or damage caused, or alleged to have been caused, directly or indirectly, by the information contained in this book.

PRAISE FOR THE BOOK

"Ian Fisher has produced a comprehensive and eminently useful volume. Anyone contemplating entering the Information Technology workplace, and even those already there, will benefit from this thoughtfully considered and beautifully organized guidebook that addresses every relevant topic, including a frank discussion of outsourcing and its impact on the IT job market. Enthusiastically recommended."
>Dennis Green, Director
>Information Technology programs
>Columbia University - School of Continuing Education

"Ian Fisher's new book is an indispensable compass for those beginning their career journey into the largely-uncharted information technology field. Like the best maps and field guides, it provides a complete and clear exploration of the varied and often confusing IT terrain--from identifying the personal skills prerequisite for different IT career paths to navigating the myriad IT educational and training options and ultimately arriving successfully at that first position. Don't leave "home" without it!
>Dr. Richard Vigilante, Executive Director
>Jesuit Distance Education Network
>New York, NY

"Very few people consciously select their careers. Most start a profession without really understanding the associated field, responsibilities, compensation, and sacrifices; this is especially true in the volatile Information Technology industry. Ian Fisher's excellent "How to Start a Career in Information Technology", provides step-by-step guidance on making that choice, from exploring the basic question of "Is a career in Information Technology right for me?" to presenting suggestions on how to find one's first IT position. It comes highly recommended."

> Cynthia Cravens, Director
> Information Technology Program
> Jewish Vocational Services
> San Francisco, CA

"Ian Fisher's book 'How to Start a Career in Information Technology' is an excellent resource to anyone considering a career in the IT field. The High Tech world is here to stay. This book provides the kind of information needed for the prospective techie. Many schools and programs offer IT training; this book teaches how to target your interests, and develop that interest into an IT career."

> L'esa Guilian, Ph.D.
> Director, Human Resources
> California Institute of Integral Studies
> San Francisco, CA

"A great source and step-by-step guide to the career assessment and job search process. This book is an easy read and the ideas can be readily implemented"

> Dr. Lois Blades-Rosado, Executive Director
> State University of New York-Brooklyn
> Educational Opportunity Center
> Brooklyn, NY

"This book written on the field of Information Technology, is one of the best resources of its kind on this field of work. Mr. Fisher has concentrated on this one career area in a very thorough fashion. The book gives the user ideas and information on the pluses and minuses of a bachelor's degree vs. a certificate, and how this may impact earnings potential. It is very non-judgmental regarding education requirements, and shows that there are possibilities in IT at every education level from certificate through a baccalaureate degree. I think anyone who is thinking of IT as a possible career will find this book extremely useful."

M. Sumyyah Bilal
Chief Executive Officer
EUREKA, CCIS
Richmond, CA

"Should be required reading for anyone contemplating an IT career. Presents complicated information in a clear, interesting, and concise manner. Reader-friendly, demystifying, thoughtful, practical..."

Merble Reagon, Executive Director
The Women's Center for Education and Career Advancement
New York City

TABLE OF CONTENTS

PREFACE

"U.S. software programmers' career prospects, once dazzling, are now in doubt. Just look at global giants, from IBM and Electronic Data Systems to Lehman Brothers and Merrill Lynch. They're rushing to hire tech workers offshore while liquidating thousands of jobs in America. In the past three years, offshore programming jobs have nearly tripled, from 27,000 to an estimated 80,000, according to Forrester Research Inc." [1]

The topic of IT employment would not be complete without a discussion of outsourcing and off-shoring. I will first attempt to briefly define outsourcing and off-shoring, then discuss how to protect your job. The issue of American jobs is always a highly charged topic, especially so in an election year such as this is. There is so much rhetoric about this issue that it is sometimes hard to get a good understanding of what the issues are. With a basic understanding of the forces at work, one can undertake specific steps to protect ones career and livelihood. We will start by talking about globalization which is the context within which outsourcing and off-shoring exist.

Globalization

Today large multinationals operate in many countries. These companies buy and sell goods and services all over the world and are no longer loyal to a particular state or country. They answer to their shareholders. These companies pay taxes to governments and wages to employees in many countries, making them a very potent political force in the countries in which they operate. Most governments welcome large multinationals with open arms for the jobs they will create and the taxes they will pay.

Some say globalization is bad for workers because a company can easily move an entire division to another country if labor (or other) costs are deemed too high. Supporters of globalization say it helps companies to compete, by freeing them to pursue opportunities that ultimately benefit shareholders and customers.

Outsourcing

> "...whether you know it or not, when you call Delta Airlines, American Express, Sprint, Citibank, IBM or Hewlett Packard's technical support number, chances are you'll be talking to an Indian." [2]

Outsourcing is when an organization decides to contract-out; typically for business services that were traditionally performed in-house. Outsourcing today is often in the area of services: call center, data processing, debt collection, to name a few. In about 1990 the recent outsourcing phenomena began in earnest. Large multinationals such as Kodak, began outsourcing significant parts of their IT operations.[3] In some cases outsourcing contracts went to

American companies (IBM in the case of Kodak) sometimes they went to foreign firms. Due to the political uproar that resulted, many companies wanted to keep quiet about it. According to the CIO of a major Fortune 100 manufacturer "We don't want a situation where the public sees us as a malevolent force and takes it out on our products." [4]

Nonetheless by the year 2000 "outsourcing has exploded into a $100 billion (and growing) global industry" and is predicted to reach $151 billion by 2003, according to International Data Corporation. [5]

Off-Shoring

> "The call center employees earn $3,000 to $5,000 a year, in a nation where the per capita income is less than $500." [6]

Off-shoring is a derivative of outsourcing whereby the services are performed overseas by a foreign company using foreign employees. Off-shoring is a more recent phenomenon and poses a more direct threat to U.S. jobs. When a job is off-shored it leaves this country, which means it is not being done by an American worker. Instead of company X (U.S. company) paying a worker a salary of Y, they are paying a foreign firm. This is sort of a double negative for the U.S. economy. A worker is displaced, and a foreign company is getting paid. Why do organizations choose to off-shore?:

SAVE MONEY: An organization reduces its workforce by sending a project, process, or service, off-shore

STRATEGIC: An organization chooses to augment a project, process, or service through the use of off-shore workers

ADDED CAPACITY: An organization wants to add a specific capability, process, or service, presumably one it does not already have; it acquires this capability off-shore

The Debate

> "Bangalore, India, may be on the verge of overtaking Silicon Valley as home to the world's largest concentration of technology workers, as U.S. companies expand their use of offshore workers" [7]

Workers and labor unions feel outsourcing and off-shoring puts U.S. IT jobs at risk. Large multinationals feel they must compete using all the tools at their disposal. There is truth to both sides, U.S. jobs are being lost and many multinationals seek to maximize shareholder value through outsourcing and off shoring. Are U.S. jobs more important than corporate profit? The equation is complex and depends from which side you are viewing the debate. As a shareholder, I may feel differently than as a worker. As a consumer I may feel that lower prices are more important than protecting American jobs.

How to Protect your Job

Outsourcing is really not something you can be protected against. An organization may choose to outsource almost any particular business function. Almost everyone is vulnerable to some degree. I will focus more on how to protect ones job from the more recent phenomena; off-shoring.

Political pressure

Raise your concerns with your elected officials. Let them know you are concerned about this issue. If there is no political pressure off-shoring of IT jobs will accelerate further.

Keep your IT skills current

Most new technology still originates here in the United States. As a result, use this to your advantage. Try to learn and use the latest technology. Consider one of the relevant IT certifications if it will show your skills are up to date.

Read the news

Read the business/labor news in particular. Keep abreast of the larger issues that affect not just your industry, but others as well. Having a well rounded understanding of the forces affecting business in general, will help you to prepare for the latest developments. To be forewarned is to be forearmed.

Pay close attention to your industry and your company/organization

Read widely within your own industry, don't be the last one to know. Understand your industry and the challenges it faces. The same applies to the organization you work for.

Consider management

Managers have institutional knowledge that makes them difficult to replace. Typically management is not often something that is off-shored. Consider moving into an IT management position as it may provide additional job security.

Consider occupations that do not lend themselves to off-shoring

Consider working in areas of the economy less likely to off shore jobs: government or education for example. In the IT field some occupations are less vulnerable to off shoring, for example: help desk, network administration, and computer training. Think of positions where the work must be performed locally at the work site.

INTRODUCTION

Why this book?

It is clear to me that many people [desperately] need career and life planning skills. We must all learn these skills somehow and use them over our lifetimes. Unfortunately, our educational system does little to teach these skills, at least not in any systematic way. In America, grades one through 12 are compulsory, after which we are asked to choose a career and go on to college. If during those 12 years we have not developed some career and life planning skills, we do not have the knowledge to make good career choices. If we have no idea before college what profession we would like to enter, then college becomes an expensive process of exploration. The value of a college education would be greatly enhanced if those arriving knew ahead of time the direction they want to go.

This book grew out of a seminar that I began teaching in 1990 at Long Island University in Brooklyn, NY.

At the time I was managing a wide array of non-credit certificate programs for working adults in the Information Technology area (IT). Each semester a significant number of new students would see me for career advice. Most of them asked how much money they could earn in the field upon graduation. They also asked which certificate would give them the best chance of getting a job. I quickly realized many of them had little or no idea how to choose a career, whether in IT or any other field. For most, the primary concern was how much money they could make. Few had any concept of the particular careers and almost none had considered whether they would enjoy a career in IT, much less whether they'd be good at it. The most common questions were:

- How much money can I make?
- Do I have what it takes? What aptitudes are needed?
- Is this a growing field?
- How do I choose a particular specialization within the IT field?
- What kind of training/education do I need?
- What are employers looking for?

My meetings with the students usually consisted of my telling them not to base career decisions solely on money, and to find out as much as possible about the field before deciding on a new career, or committing to a training program. It is clear to me there is a need for career and life planning skills for those considering IT careers.

What I hope to accomplish

In this book I hope to provide a roadmap for those wishing to start careers in Information Technology. I hope to accomplish this by:

- Helping readers determine whether IT is the field for them

- Offering suggestions on how to choose an area of specialization
- Helping readers develop a network of industry contacts
- Providing the latest statistics on job growth in the IT field
- Helping readers make informed educational choices
- Providing unbiased information about IT careers and how to obtain them
- Providing input from industry professionals

HOW WE CHOOSE OUR CAREERS

Friends, Family

Most of us choose our careers based in part on the advice of our friends and family. If these influential people have our best interests at heart, this can be fine. But because our friends and family are people we trust, almost implicitly, we must use caution to balance their opinions against our own. This is not always easy. We have all heard stories of children who follow their parent's career path only to find it completely unsuitable for them. In some cases, our family determines what we will study. If the family has a business sometimes the children follow their parents into it. In some cases, the oldest child follows the father into the same line of work, and some families dictate to the children what they should study. Sometimes the influence is more subtle; there may be an unspoken expectation that the children will become doctors or lawyers. The influence of family on one's choice of career can be quite powerful. Another powerful influence is that of one's friends.

Very often our friends have a similar ability to influence our decision making. Usually they are the people we turn to for advice on any important decision.

Friends and family certainly should be a part of your decision-making process, but don't blindly follow their recommendations or suggestions. So while you should get as many opinions as possible on your career choice, you should not depend solely upon friends and family for career advice or direction. Remember that they may not have the information needed to provide good advice, and may also have their own motives.

News media

The news media and popular press are sources where many of us get our information about the labor market. It is an excellent source of late breaking news and information. The popular press can be a good source of predictions for the direction of the labor market however, the information is usually very superficial, with little explanation of the underlying assumptions, or subsequent conclusions. Most labor market information comes from the government, specifically the U.S. Department of Labor – Bureau of Labor Statistics (BLS). The popular press bases much of its labor market reporting on government research. Why? Because it's easy – the work has already been done and it's free. Because much of labor market reporting comes from the government, usually they are seen as the authority. This can be a problem when the government's understanding of a particular industry is less than satisfactory, or plain wrong. I have watched the BLS track job growth in the IT industry for the past 15-years; and while their coverage of the industry has definitely improved, I still find assumptions and statements I disagree with.

For example, the way they categorize IT occupations is highly questionable. They gather information on an occupation called Computer Systems Analysts, a job posting you will never see in the real world, for the terminology is inappropriate. The government uses a terminology all its own, which sometimes has no bearing on the real world of IT. They have a wide territory to cover, and sometimes don't have resources or staff to cover it sufficiently well. In order to make the best use of BLS resources, one has to read their research closely and understand the assumptions they make. Another fact should be kept in mind: the government will not track a particular occupation until it is sufficient in number to justify such tracking. This means that fast growing new occupations do not show up on their radar for a while. Positions like "webmaster" or "web application developer" for example, are still not on the government's radar. To bring this point home, just think the whole dot com craze came and went, and the government never picked those jobs up on its radar. I am amazed that such an important part of the economy and workforce could be so completely ignored. Because the government is tracking such a wide range of occupations, they only know so much about any particular one. When relying on the popular press, be sure to check the sources of their information, and do not simply take what they say at face value. The popular press tends to sensationalize as a way to sell. The press also tends to simplify things; understanding labor markets is anything but simple. When evaluating BLS information, realize that their understanding of the industry is not always accurate or complete. Look for alternate sources.

What's hot or trendy

At different times certain careers become trendy. There was a time in the late nineties when "webmaster" was one of the most fashionable careers. It seemed like almost every technology magazine had a cover with some young twenty something making a six-figure salary with millions in stock options. Wow, how times have changed! Most of these people are now out of work.

For awhile, physical therapy was hot, as was special education. The list goes on. The point here is not to ride the wave with whatever is trendy. What goes up must come down. Make your choice of a career based on what you enjoy, the money will follow. When researching "trendy" careers, make sure to do your research, check the facts. Find out what the underlying assumptions are. Check multiple sources. Understand what that job feels like, the everyday. Do not limit yourself to library research; get out into the field. Of course, making good career choices requires trial and error. It is a learning process. Making good career choices requires gathering as much information as possible. It requires as clear an understanding of the chosen occupation as possible. That should be your goal.

> "I'd say about half of the students I see are searching for a major or a career direction. Counselors, however, see only those who acknowledge they don't know; I think many students make choices for the wrong reasons: the main ones being parental pressure, desire for financial gain, status, what's "hot"
>
> - Karin C. Nelson, Career Counselor at San Francisco City College

Questions to ask yourself

- What forces influenced (or are influencing) you in choosing your career?

- How did you arrive at your choice of a career; what process did you use to decide?
- What were the factors that affected your decision?

Summary

- Understand and balance the influences (friends, family, media, your research) bearing on your career decision
- Use the popular press with caution
- Make good choices by gathering as much information as possible

HOW WE SHOULD CHOOSE OUR CAREERS

Now that you know some of the pitfalls about choosing careers, let us focus on more effective methods. Choosing a major or career is an exciting process that can greatly impact the rest of your life! "Career planning" is an intentional process that helps make sure your choices are indeed informed, and not random last-minute decisions.

Learn about yourself

It is ironic that a career search starts inside, with you. Most people do everything but look into themselves. A career search can never be successful unless you first look inside yourself. Why? Because your ultimate satisfaction depends on you and no one else. You ultimately must determine what success or happiness means to you. Not only do you have to create a picture of career success, you must also determine when you have become successful. These are not easy things to do; they are things that we must constantly revisit throughout our lives.

- Do I like working with people?
- Do I like working with things?
- Do I like working alone?

These few questions should start you on a journey toward finding the best career for you. The demographers today predict that the average American will have three to six careers in his or her lifetime. Do not become paralyzed about making your career decision; you will most likely have other careers in your lifetime. Take a deep breath and rest easy. Go back in your life to the times when you were happiest, to the activities that you enjoy most. Were those activities mostly with others? Do you like tinkering, or working with your hands? Do you like solitude and working alone? What subjects did you enjoy most in school? Only you can answer these questions, and you must, in order to choose the best career for you. If you are logical and analytical, and enjoy working alone, maybe computer programming would be a good career for you. Start by asking yourself these questions, and reflecting back upon your life. The self-assessment chapter will revisit these questions.

Select an industry or occupation

The IT profession is enormous, with many specializations, therefore; First let us define Information Technology. The U.S. Department of Commerce in its report "Digital Economy 2002" defines workers in information technology as those "who design, manufacture, operate, maintain, and repair Information Technology products and provide related services across all industries." Your first step is to learn as much as possible about the industry. BLS estimates there are approximately 3.3 million information technology workers. This number

excludes marketing and sales workers employed by
Information Technology companies. BLS categorizes
these workers into 12 groups that are tracked using
Standard Occupational Classification System (SOC)
codes. The 12 groups are:

- Computer and information systems managers
- Computer programmers
- Computer and information scientists
- Computer systems analysts
- Computer hardware engineers
- Computer software engineers, applications
- Computer Software engineers, systems software
- Computer support specialists
- Database administrators
- Network and computer systems administrators
- Network systems and data communications analysts
- All other computer specialists, a residual category of workers

The list above should give you a jumping off point
for further research into these occupations; point
your browser to: www.bls.gov. Your reading should
be general so you get a sense of the industry as a
whole. When you find an area of the industry that
interests you, focus in that area. Find out which
companies are the major players in your industry.
Find out who the major manufacturers are, the
software developers, and the major service firms. As
you begin to educate yourself, you will find areas of
the industry that interest you; Pursue them. Research
a few of the occupations that interest you. The IT
field is too large for generalists; you must focus on a
particular occupation. You can change later, if you
don't like what you find out. Below are some of the
more popular occupations:

- Help Desk/User Support

These are the folks who provide support to employees of most medium to large organizations. They go out on "calls" to help employees with computer problems. Support people are always on the go. They are rarely at their desks. Computer support people must do a fair amount of physical lifting and moving of equipment. Of the computer professions, this is probably the most physically demanding.

Technical skills a help desk person should have: a solid understanding of operating systems, personal computer hardware knowledge, personal computer application software skills.

Transferable skills a help desk person should have: helping, communicating, analyzing, instructing, interpreting, listening, problem-solving, upgrading, reasoning, memorizing, lifting, understanding, ascertaining, fixing, diagnosing, installing.

- Database development

Database developers are responsible for designing and/or maintaining databases for medium to large size companies. In some companies database design is handled by one person or group, and the maintenance and fine tuning is handled by another person or group. In a smaller company, the same person may perform both functions. A database developer must understand the information needs of an organization. Normally, a database is designed to automate a particular business function within an organization. The developer must understand that particular business function. [In many cases the developer is automating a function that has been performed manually.] Depending on the size of the company, a database developer may work alone or with others. In larger companies a database developer would be part of a team. This team would interact with other teams, for example, programmers, or application developers. They would also interact with the systems people, and the data center. A database developer must understand the operating system on which they are working; examples are: Unix, Windows, Linux, MVS, or VMS. The database developer must understand in great detail the software used to develop the database; for example: Oracle, Sybase, SAS, Informix, SQL/SQL server, CICS, IMS.

Technical skills a database developer should have: a solid understanding of the operating system for the chosen development platform, personal computer application software skills, and programming skills. Obviously the database developer must understand in great detail the software used to develop the database.

Transferable skills a database developer should have: analyzing, calculating, checking, classifying, collecting, compiling, computing, coding, designing, developing, diagnosing, estimating, evaluating, extracting, formulating, fixing, gathering, generating, interpreting, manipulating, modeling, ordering, predicting, programming, researching, sorting, solving, testing & proving.

- Programming

Programmers write the software that computers run in order to perform their various functions. Software is the set of instructions that tells the computer what to do. Programmers write software using many different languages such as: Visual C++, Pascal, HTML, XML, COBOL, Java/JavaScript, to name few. Programmers eventually specialize in a particular area, or on a particular platform. Some programmers specialize in writing software for large mainframe computers such as IBM, while others write software for microcomputers such as the Apple or the personal computer running Windows. Some programmers specialize in writing programs for the web, some write operating system utilities, and others may write accounting software. As you can see, programming is a huge field. Despite this fact, the tasks are basically the same: flowcharting, using structured programming techniques, coding, testing, and debugging.

Technical skills a programmer should have: a solid understanding of the operating system for the chosen development platform, personal computer application software skills, and the ability to work with abstract concepts. Programmers also must have a detailed knowledge of the programming language they are working with.

Transferable skills a programmer should have: analyzing, calculating, checking, classifying, collecting, compiling, computing, coding, designing, developing, diagnosing, estimating, editing, evaluating, organizing, fixing, gathering, generating, interpreting, manipulating, modeling, ordering, predicting, programming, researching, sorting, solving, testing & proving.

- Web Application Development

Typically web application development involves everything needed to create a fully functioning web site. A web developer must know how to design a web page graphically. The developer must also know how to program the web page to perform any necessary functions or calculations. For example, a web page may be required to calculate sales tax. Such a calculation requires some programming know-how. As you can see, the functional boundaries can become blurred between a programmer and web application developer. The developer must also understand how the web page behaves on the client PC. In addition, the developer must understand the functions of the web server. The most common are: the Internet Information Server (IIS) from Microsoft, and the Apache web server from Linux. Other software/languages that a web application developer may use are: Perl, HTML, Apache Web Server, IIS, ASP, XML, CGI, Director, Dreamweaver, Flash, FrontPage, HTML, Illustrator. A web server is the repository of all the pages and content of a web site.

Technical skills a web application developer should have: a solid understanding of the operating system for the chosen development platform, personal computer application software skills, programming skills, and, probably most importantly, knowledge of the web server.

Transferable skills a web application developer should have: analyzing, calculating, checking, classifying, collecting, compiling, computing, coding, designing, developing, diagnosing, estimating, editing, evaluating, organizing, fixing, integrating, gathering, generating, interpreting, manipulating, modeling, ordering, predicting, programming, presenting, researching, sorting, solving, testing & proving.

- Networking

Networking, or network administration, is another very large area like programming, with many specializations and sub-specializations. Some networking professionals work exclusively on large mainframe networks such as an IBM MVS environment. Such an environment is quite different from a small Local Area Network of PCs connected together. Most networking jobs involve supporting personal computer networks that run Novell or Microsoft operating systems. A networking professional is involved with a wide range of both hardware and software tasks: installing software, configuring software, adding and deleting users, installing network cards, installing printers, installing personal computers, running cable, and installing RAM memory. A network administrator must have a good understanding of the network operating system (NOS). A solid knowledge of personal computer hardware is also required. Maintaining a network requires hardware, software, and operating system knowledge. A typical network involves both the clients and a server or servers. A server is a powerful computer used to store the data and programs needed by users. A network administrator must be knowledgeable in how to set up and maintain a server.

Technical skills a network administrator should have: a solid understanding of personal computer hardware, the client operating system, and the NOS, personal computer application software skills.

Transferable skills a web application developer should have: problem solving, lifting, analyzing, communicating, inspecting, diagnosing, checking, implementing, fixing, helping, improving, influencing, explaining, expanding, estimating, integrating, investigating, observing, planning, problem-solving, reasoning, solving, trouble-shooting, upgrading, repairing.

The above-mentioned list is merely a starting point showing you the larger areas of specialization where most jobs fall. Most IT jobs involve one or more of the areas mentioned above. Pick an area that seems interesting to you and begin researching it. In the beginning there is so much to learn. Do not stress over this. As you learn more about the industry, your likes and dislikes will guide you. Most often the paralysis you may feel in choosing an area of specialization results from a lack of information. As you learn more about the industry, your aptitudes and instincts will guide you. No matter how you choose, you should continue to narrow your focus. Select an initial area that seems appealing and begin to research it further.

Talk to people in the industry

"Begin developing a network of contacts. There is no better way to begin to learn what IT is all about than to talk to folks with experience in the field. Many IT workers and managers will take the time to talk to folks starting out. Start with friends and family; chances are they may have a friend or acquaintance in the IT field."

- Mark Butler, Business Development Director, Bay Area Technology Education Collaborative

One of the best ways to find out if you enjoy a particular kind of work is to go to work with someone who does that job. For example, let's suppose I would like to become a computer programmer; in order to do so I need to understand what a programmer does. Assuming I know little about what programmers do, it would be very beneficial to talk to someone who is a programmer. Maybe I have a family member or a distant cousin I can call on. Maybe I have a friend in computers, and maybe he or she works with programmers. What I would like to do is talk with this person, and maybe visit their worksite. There is nothing more valuable in your job search than having first-hand knowledge of the job you're going after. Conversely, there is nothing worse than finding out that the job you have trained for is not something you enjoy. Too many people base their career choice on hunches, newspaper articles, or someone's advice. Do not make this mistake. If you want to become a programmer, go and talk to two or three people who are programmers. Maybe take them to lunch. Ask whether they enjoy their careers, and how they got started. Share your concerns about choosing a new career, and ask them for advice. Ask what a typical day looks like. If after talking with them you are still not sure what being a programmer is like, offer to volunteer. Perform any task that would allow you to be around programmers. Get coffee and donuts in the morning. Sharpen pencils. This is an excellent way to get an inside look at the world of programmers. Doing research up front will help avoid disappointment later. Most people in the industry love to talk shop and you can take advantage of this. Most IT professionals would love to help a dedicated newcomer enter the field. Most of us are full of advice and would love to share it.

Take a class

For those with little or no technical knowledge, I highly recommend taking some short introductory classes. Enroll in a short computer class for the purpose of getting an introduction to the subject, and to have access to the instructor. Ask the instructor for advice in selecting your career. Ask about their background and how they got started. Instructors are a wonderful resource, and they are usually excellent communicators who enjoy sharing information. In a short period of time, and for little expense, you will gain valuable knowledge and learn about possible career choices. Universities and colleges are also excellent places to obtain career information, if you know how to find it. Make an appointment to talk with the chairman of computer science, and ask him/her for help choosing a career. Attend open houses and information sessions for new students. Typically these are offered each semester through appropriate academic departments, or through adult education (sometimes called extended education or extension).

Most universities have career counselors; make use of them. They are usually found in the career planning and placement office at most colleges and universities. Go to the campus library, and ask for the career section. Speak with the librarian about what you are looking for. Read trade magazines that are appropriate for the occupation you have chosen.

My first contact with computers was in 1981 at college, when I took my first computer class called CS 561 Computer Graphics. We learned graphics programming on 64k Apple II's; Imagine that! I absolutely loved it, so much so that I joined the computer society at my college! This chance encounter changed my life significantly, though I did not know it at the time.

It is important for you to make contact with people who are in the industry; in the early stages of choosing a career this is especially important. Speaking to people in the industry is essential to your career success. What they tell you will be invaluable. Keep in touch with them as your career develops, for they may become an important source of job leads or other important information. Taking a class is an excellent way of meeting someone in the industry.

Ask yourself -- Would I like doing this?

"You start instead by doing some hard homework on yourself, first doing a thorough inventory of what skills you most enjoy using; and then doing a thorough inventory of where you want to use those skills." [8]

After having talked to some professionals, and taken a class or two, you should have a sense of what direction to go in, at least initially. Remember not to fret too much over your initial career choice, for it may change. Let's suppose you have decided to become a programmer. You like what you have seen so far and feel this would be a good fit for you. At this point I would make a few suggestions. First, I would recommend your buying a compiler and a few books and start programming. An inexpensive basic compiler can be had for less than $100; a couple of used books can be had for less than $50. Write dozens of programs and show them to your professional contacts.

Utilize every method you can think of to better inform yourself about what you're getting into. The more research you do on your future occupation, the better prepared you will be. Making poor career choices leads to unnecessary frustration. In my experience most people make bad career choices because of a lack of good information, and poor planning.

Assess your aptitudes and what you enjoy doing

"Take an IT class to see how they like it. I remember trying to take FORTRAN in college and being bored to death. When students say, "I want to study computers," I always ask why. If they say "Because that's where the jobs are" (though not recently), I ask them, "How do you know you'll like IT work or be successful at it?" I dig for their real interests and talents and try to steer them that way, telling them that they'll be more successful if they follow their interests and talents rather than the money trail."

- Karin C. Nelson, Career Counselor at San
Francisco City College

Assuming you are now somewhat familiar with
computer programming, how does it feel? Does it suit
you? Do you like sitting in front of a computer all
day? Does it seem difficult? Do you enjoy writing
programs? If sparks are not flying, then maybe this is
not the area for you. Most of us, when we have found
our calling, are ecstatic! If not, don't despair; there
are many other areas to explore. Do not
underestimate your initial impressions; they are
critical. Unfortunately, many of us do not trust our
instincts as much as we should. If it does not feel
right, it probably isn't. Fortunately, there are a
number of tools that can help us get a handle on what
our aptitudes are. Below is a brief list:

Strong Interest Inventory (SII)

www.cpp.com Note: there is a charge to purchase the
SII online. The SII is based on the idea that
individuals are more satisfied and productive when
they work in jobs or at tasks that they find
interesting, and when they work with people whose
interests are similar to their own. The SII takes about
25 minutes to complete and contains 317 items that
measure your interests in a wide range of occupations,
occupational activities, hobbies, leisure activities and
types of people. Your interests are compared to
thousands of individuals who report being happy and
successful in their jobs. Your personalized report
identifies your optimum career choices based on your
interests and includes additional related occupations
with concise job descriptions. The SII can be used in
the following situations:
• People considering a career change
• Employees seeking more satisfying work within an
organization

• Students exploring career options
• Organizations looking to retain star performers and key staff
• Midlife and older adults planning their retirement

Myers-Briggs Type Indicator (MBTI)

www.mbti.com Note: there is a charge to purchase the MBTI online. The Myers-Briggs Personality Type Indicator® is a questionnaire based on the psychological teachings of Carl Gustav Jung. He is one of the founders of modern psychoanalytical theory and practice. This indicator has been developed over 35 years of rigorous scientific validation and is the most widely used of any personality indicator. The main points to understand are: The indicator is a useful tool to enlarge and deepen our self-knowledge and understanding of our behavior. It can be of real benefit to us in making informed life-choices, and in relationship building. Some people may at first be skeptical about the usefulness of the indicator. Myers-Briggs has been rigorously tried and validated over decades of refinement, by highly qualified personnel. It is not a test. There are no right or wrong answers. The MBTI® instrument determines preferences on four dichotomies:

• Extraversion–Introversion: describes where people prefer to focus their attention and get their energy—from the outer world of people and activity or their inner world of ideas and experiences
• Sensing–Intuition: describes how people prefer to take in information—focused on what is real and actual or on patterns and meanings in data
• Thinking–Feeling: describes how people prefer to make decisions—based on logical analysis or guided by concern for their impact on others

• Judging–Perceiving: describes how people prefer to deal with the outer world—in a planned orderly way, or in a flexible spontaneous way

SIGI Plus®

www.ets.org/sigi Note: there may be a charge to purchase SIGI online. Educational and career planning software integrates self-assessment with in-depth and up-to-date career information. It is easy to use, and provides a realistic view of the best educational and career options. The program is based on Educational Testing Service (ETS) research, is updated annually, and provides links to the best educational and career planning Web sites available. SIGI PLUS for Windows and the Internet are licensed nationwide to institutions, states, one-stop career centers, libraries, and community-based organizations, and others. ETS offers this product to help you better prepare for tomorrow, today.

EUREKA

www.eureka.org Note: there is no charge for this service.
The first key component of the job search process is to assess your skills, preferences, and even your personality. To assist you in this self-discovery process, we offer the following tools:
• True Colors: True Colors is a personality-based self-assessment tool that is fun, easy to use, yet extremely insightful. The assessment is based on your selecting keywords that are descriptive of your personality characteristics. The key words are age appropriate. The results gives you a four color profile and a list of occupations that are compatible with your color.
• MicroSkills: enables you to view yourself from a transferable skills or talent perspective. Everyone has some natural abilities. So, even if you have never held a job, or gone to college, you have skills that are used

on a day to day basis. MicroSkills helps you to discover what those skills are and how they can be used in the world or work. This on-line skills assessment has two options, a card sort and a questionnaire. You can save your sessions and come back at a later date to complete them. Skills results are motivational and informative.

What do you like to do? What are you good at? Before deciding on a new career, it is worthwhile to spend some time thinking about these questions. When I decided on a career in computers, I took a class to find out more about it. I enjoyed it, in part because I had always liked machines and pushing buttons. Don't overlook such seemingly trivial details, for they say a lot about you and your aptitudes or likes. Many people give too much weight to salaries when choosing a new career. We must think first about our own aptitudes and skills; money will come if we enjoy our job and do it well over time.

> "...know yourself by doing a thorough self-assessment; begin exploration by researching, reading (books, newspaper, college catalogues), using the computer, and above all, doing information interviews with people who are doing jobs you think you'd like. Volunteering or getting a gofer part-time job is a fabulous way both to try out a career direction or industry, and gain experience."

> - Karin C. Nelson, Career Counselor at San Francisco City College

One way to do this is to think back to things that you enjoyed, perhaps a class you took. Or maybe a movie that you saw got you thinking about a new career. Maybe a friend had a job that seemed appealing. This is how we start to think about our own aptitudes. An aptitude is simply something we enjoy and are good at; the two go hand-in-hand. The more time we spend thinking about our aptitudes, the better informed we will be about the best career for us. It makes no sense to make a career choice based simply upon where the money is. This is a recipe for disaster, because in all likelihood, at some point you will become unhappy with your career choice. Why? Because you left yourself out of the process of choosing! It's better to spend some time in the beginning stages of your career search, think about what you enjoy, and discern what you have been good at in the past. (The next chapter will get you started.) If you like working with people, you may want to consider IT training, for example. If you're the solitary type, programming may be more appropriate for you. Utilize, as mentioned earlier, MBTI or SII, to help you find your aptitudes.

> "Huge life decisions often are made in the whim of a moment. This is, indeed, the way most career choices (and career changes) are made. No wonder surveys of worker dissatisfaction find that up to 80%, or four out of every five workers, are dissatisfied with some important aspects of their jobs or careers. It's not a pretty picture." [9]

It may be helpful to talk with a guidance counselor if you are in high school or college, or even if you are not. If not, there are career counselors available to the public through state run workforce development agencies. Visit the web site for the state you live in. It can be quite helpful to talk over your plans with a knowledgeable professional. Having a sounding board can be quite helpful. You need someone to bounce your ideas off of, someone to hear you out. Making career choices should not be done in a vacuum, you need to involve other people. Talk with your friends, family, and co-workers. Guidance counselors are often an excellent resource and can be quite helpful in assisting you with locating resources. A tremendous resource for helping assess aptitudes is Richard Nelson Bolles book, "What Color is your Parachute?" this book is the bible of career and life planning, and has been published continuously for more than 20 years. In the book you'll find exercises that will help you determine and assess your aptitudes. You will also find a chapter on career counselors, and how to find them and work with them. There are also exercises you can take to help determine what you might like, or be good at.

> "Take some courses and see if you like it. Technical careers tend to work best for highly logical thinkers and people who enjoy working by themselves. If you don't like the courses, consider the possibility that IT may not be a good choice for you. Also, bear in mind that "IT" is a multi-faceted career. Programming and systems administration are only two. What they all have in common is a technical basis and the ability to function as part of a team working to build a product."
>
> - Philip Laird, Computer Scientist and Teacher

Determine what the employment outlook is

Typically you plan for a career with growth potential. It is very easy to find out about the growth potential for a new career, you just have to know where to look. Many people leave out this very important step in changing careers, or starting a new one. While you should choose with your heart, research with your head. We often make career decisions with little or no concrete information; this is a shame because there's so much good information available free of charge. The job outlook for the IT field as a whole is promising, and the statistics bear this out. (Refer to the Charts and Tables section at the end of this book.)

Questions to ask yourself

- Do you know what type of working environment you would like/dislike?
- Do you like working alone, or with others?
- Which IT careers seem interesting to you?
- Ask yourself, "would I like this?"
- What are the day-to-day duties?
- What is the salary range?
- What is the current and future job outlook?
- What training is needed to work in this field?
- What certificates or degrees are required to work in this field?
- What does the coursework really involve?
- Are the duties of the position tasks that you enjoy?
- What skills, interests, values, and personality types excel in this career?
- What values are important to you in the workplace?

Summary

- Learn about yourself
- Select an industry or occupation and learn about it
- Talk to people in the occupation you have chosen
- Take a class to learn what the work is like
- Assess your aptitudes
- Determine the employment outlook of the specialization you've chosen

SELF ASSESSMENT

Let us now look inward at ourselves. Career and life planning is by its very nature an internal process. For many, job hunting becomes a time of soul searching because many of us take the opportunity to think of a new career. Or, we may take the opportunity to evaluate how satisfying (or not) our current career is. Often, a job hunt is much more than simply looking for another job, it is often a re-evaluation of our current career. For some reason, many of us don't feel worthy, or entitled to enjoy our lives! When I was a kid work always seemed like something you had to do, enjoyment was never part of the equation. For many immigrant families and families of color this is particularly true; as it is for the generation that survived the Great Depression in this country (as my father did) in 1929. Many of us have adopted this attitude that looks at work as a burden, something unpleasant we must do. This is not the way it has to be, we can enjoy our work, in fact we should, we must. All it takes is doing our homework. I assure you if each of us spent as much time each week on our careers, as we do on our laundry, we would all be much happier in our careers and therefore in our lives.

The self assessment is an essential part of every job hunt, or career change. It is the fun part, where we get to explore all our options, consider all possibilities. A career self assessment is asking ourselves "What do I like doing? What am I good at? What do I enjoy? Where do I want to go with my life?" We need to do this because:

- We often leave ourselves out of the equation when choosing a new job/career
- We need to understand what motivates and inspires us
- We need to understand what skills we already possess
- We need to determine a plan of action

What transferable skills do you already have?

Transferable skills are those skills we all have but are rarely aware of. Experts say that 70% of our skills are transferable, meaning we can take them with us to our next job or career. This should be good news to all job seekers. Though we rarely realize it, most of the skills we will need we already have. The seven step self assessment (page 100) will help you to realize what transferable skills you have, and enjoy using. This will provide the springboard for deciding what is next for you. The reason for doing the self assessment is to find out what skills you have, and enjoy using. This is an important and revealing exercise. You will learn things about yourself you did not know, and you will begin to realize the tremendous number of options open to you in your quest for meaningful work. You will find out not only what skills you possess, but which ones you enjoy using most. By doing this you are learning about yourself and what you enjoy in the world of work. This information will help you to uncover new opportunities in your job/career hunt. To get a better idea of what transferable skills are, look at page 109. If you would like, take a moment and complete the self assessment that starts on page 100.

Identify your occupation and your field

In order to understand where you have been it helps to break things down by occupation and field. It is part of understanding what you do, and where you are doing it. This helps tremendously in two ways: 1. helping to understand where you may want to go next, and 2. analyzing employment and career information. If I am a teacher for example, I may want to consider changing fields maybe to health care. The health care field is growing, and there may be opportunities there for a teacher that I could explore. Having the macro view can allow you to see possibilities for career change you might not otherwise see.

In addition, the government tracks employment by occupation and field, this makes it easy for you to research and help make sound decisions on where the jobs are, and where they will be in the future. Most of us never do this when choosing careers. Looking at the world of work this way, makes it easy to make use of the wealth of information available on occupations and job growth available from the government. When contemplating a career change make sure to find out what the occupational outlook is. Where is your industry going? Is the outlook good or bad? Why? Take a look at the list of sample occupations on page 107, it should help you visualize different occupations and their associated fields.

Questions to ask yourself

- What are my top six favorite skills in order of priority?
- What skills do you enjoy using and have used in the past?
- Where would you like to use your skills?
- What is my current (or desired) occupation?
- What is the occupational outlook for my occupation?
- What is my current (or desired) field?
- What is the occupational outlook for my field?

Summary

- Understand what skills you enjoy using
- Prioritize the skills you enjoy using
- Determine your desired occupation and field, where would you like to use those skills

E DUCATION

What role does education play?

Education allows students to "try-on" different careers in a safe environment. While studying, a student is shielded somewhat from the "real world". Often undergraduates in college change majors a few times prior to graduating. Our educational system unfortunately does little to help students develop career & life planning skills.

> "I think children should be introduced to careers a lot earlier, not to make a choice, but just to learn about what kind of work people do. College is becoming increasingly expensive, making it a very expensive place to "find yourself". To make the best use of a college education, prior to arriving, one should spend a number of years considering and researching career options."
>
> - Karin C. Nelson, Career Counselor, City College of San Francisco

Another role education plays is providing basic literacy. It is crucial that the workplace, and society as a whole posses basic literacy. Basic literacy is required in all aspects of our lives. When we go to the corner store, we must be able to communicate what we want to the cashier, and we must be able to accurately count our change. When we read the daily newspaper we must be able to analyze which issues are important to us, and what action to take if any. This requires an ability to synthesize and analyze information, to think critically. Our literacy connects us to ourselves, others, and to the world. Basic literacy is far more important than any technical skills that one may develop. The ability to communicate is essential, and increases in importance the further one advances in an organization or career.

Education also can provide skills for the workplace. Formal education can provide at least two things: literacy and skills. Both basic literacy and skills are critical in the workplace. In order to enter the workforce you must be able to read, write, and speak clearly. Do not to underestimate the need for basic literacy skills. You most certainly will not be offered a job if you cannot write a basic English sentence, or a simple memo. In my many years working with students in the area of IT, I find that many want to skip the literacy and simply concentrate on technical classes. Many immigrant students (and minimally educated Americans) believe incorrectly, that only the technical skills matter. Employers look at the whole package not simply the technical skill set. Would you hire someone that does not have a strong command of the English language? How would the person interact with other staff members if they could not be easily understood? How would the supervisor handle the resulting miscommunication? Basic literacy is expected in the workplace, it is a prerequisite to any

other skill. During your formal education you'll be
exposed to basic literacy and technical skills, they are
both important.

The math myth

There is nothing more misunderstood for those
pursuing IT careers, than the "math myth". Many
people considering IT careers have a mistaken
assumption that advanced math skills are a
requirement. (By advanced math I mean beyond high
school algebra.) Unfortunately, for today's IT job
seeker this myth still persists. Many are choosing
careers other than IT, based in part on their fear of
math. Of today's IT jobs I would estimate 90% fall
into the following broad, general categories:

- Help Desk/User Support
- Database development/Administration
- Programming/Software Engineering
- Web Application Development/Graphics
- Networking/System Administration

The areas of Programming/Software Engineering
probably have the most need for advanced level math
skills. The good news is that this is just one area,
there are many others to choose from! Even within
the programming area, the need for advanced math
skills is not absolute. The need for these skills
harkens back to a time when programming tools were
more rudimentary. Code nowadays is often created via
templates, code generators, and with visual tools. As a
result, much of the drudgery that required
mathematical calculation has been eliminated. As
programming has become increasingly automated, the
need for a deep understanding of mathematics has
lessened.

Programming is a skill that is steadily being simplified
and pushed out to the masses. Macro and scripting

languages are more common than ever. As computer users increasingly demand more control, languages are being developed for them. These languages require little or no math background to manipulate successfully. The popularization of programming languages minimizes the need for math skills.

Though a small subset of all programming jobs, there are industries that require programmers with advanced math skills. Often, the type of industry or business determines the type of programming that needs to be done. Industries engaged in: technical software development, scientific research, simulation, 3d modeling, finance, statistics, or engineering, may require advanced math skills and the relevant undergraduate/graduate degrees.

If you are mathematically challenged, fear not! There are many IT careers that require little or no math!

What kind of education is needed?

There is a very useful table that maps IT careers and the suggested education needed to obtain them. See page 113. Keep in mind these are the government's best estimates, think of it as a recommendation and not as a requirement. According to the Bureau of Labor Statistics: "...in 2001 most Information Technology workers-almost 70 percent-had a bachelor's or higher degree..." It is interesting to note that "...most Information Technology workers who have a degree do not have one in a computer field." [10]

It is my feeling that a bachelor's degree is recommended to maximize ones chances for employment success in the IT field. The IT job market is becoming increasingly competitive, and there are many people unemployed job seekers with bachelor's degrees. All other things being equal they have an advantage.

> "The majority of HR executives view IT employees with college degrees as being more likely to receive multiple job offers, be hired, and be compensated at higher levels than those without college degrees. They also believe that IT employees with college degrees, compared to those without college degrees, are more productive, committed to the organization, involved in on-going learning, and likely to transfer skills learned in training to their job." [11]

It is especially true that the bachelor's degree is sometimes required for many management level job opportunities. In part this is true because there are skills required in management that, one develops while in college. The ability to think critically, to evaluate options, to synthesize information all are hallmarks of an undergraduate education. See page 120 to view a list of skills acquired during an undergraduate education.

Computer and Information Literacy

Today just about everyone understands the term computer literacy. It means understanding how to use the computer for basic tasks such as: surfing the web, writing a document, or searching a database.

The internet and other technology have helped create "information overload" whereby people are literally inundated with information. There's more information at our fingertips than ever before. Most of this information is available to us on our personal computers through the internet. As a result of technology, we now have access to unprecedented amounts of information. Anyone that has done a

Google search on the internet will be amazed at how much is available. I searched for "history of the personal computer" and received 9,640,000 hits in 0.13 seconds.

Computer literacy is more important than ever in the labor market. In most cases employer's today take for granted that job seekers know how to operate a personal computer. The ability to do a Google search is an assumed skill. For most jobs, these skills are not listed because they are taken for granted. Other skills that are often assumed include being able to successfully manipulate such software as:

- Browsers (Netscape Navigator or Microsoft's Internet Explore)
- Databases (Microsoft Access or FileMaker Pro)
- Spreadsheets (Microsoft Excel or Lotus 1-2-3)
- Word processors (Microsoft Word or Corel WordPerfect)

To be competitive in today's job market, jobseekers should be competent in using the above mentioned software applications. Computer literacy concerns itself with accessing and manipulating information. Information literacy is generally more concerned with the analysis and use of information. It is an important distinction. For example: one must know how to access and gather information (computer literacy) in order to be able to analyze it (information literacy). Academic institutions are teaching both computer literacy as well as information literacy, because they realize the need for both, not only in school but in the workplace as well. The abundance of information presents a challenge: how to effectively use all this information?

Information Literacy

Where computer literacy leaves off, information literacy begins. The definition below (italicized) is from the American Library Association: [12]

A definition

Information literacy is a set of abilities requiring individuals to "recognize when information is needed and have the ability to locate, evaluate, and use effectively the needed information." Information literacy also is increasingly important in the contemporary environment of rapid technological change and proliferating information resources. Because of the escalating complexity of this environment, individuals are faced with diverse, abundant information choices—in their academic studies, in the workplace, and in their personal lives.

The uncertain quality and expanding quantity of information pose large challenges for society. The sheer abundance of information will not in itself create a more informed citizenry without a complementary cluster of abilities necessary to use information effectively. An information literate individual is able to:

- *Determine the extent of information needed*
- *Access the needed information effectively and efficiently*
- *Evaluate information and its sources critically*
- *Incorporate selected information into one's knowledge base*
- *Use information effectively to accomplish a specific purpose*
- *Understand the economic, legal, and social issues surrounding the use of information, and access and use information ethically and legally*

Both literacy's are needed, today it is simply not enough to know how to access and manipulate information.

See page 130 for a breakdown of IT employees by
educational level. Let us now compare and contrast
the different degrees and certificates.

Associate's degree

An associate's degree is an excellent alternative to the
four year bachelor's degree. Typically an Associate's
degree is a two year degree. The Associate degree
mixes liberal arts with specific skills. It is usually a
(50/50) mixture of the skill building classes, and
liberal arts classes. This degree is usually sufficient
for entrance into an occupational field.
According to Roger Moncarz:

> "The associate degree is an increasingly
> attractive option for information technology
> workers. Most community colleges and many
> independent technical institutes and proprietary
> schools offer an associate degree in computer
> science or related information technology
> fields. But because many of these programs are
> designed to meet the needs of local businesses,
> they are more occupation-specific than are
> those of a four-year degree... There has been a
> steady rise in the number of associate degrees
> granted in the computer and information
> sciences over the last decade from fewer than
> 8,000 in 1990 to more than 20,000 in 2000." [13]

An associate's degree is sometimes called a transfer
degree, because it can be credited towards the first 2-
years of a bachelor's degree. Typically an associate's
degree requires around 60-80 credits to complete.
Associate degrees are very often vocational. Below is
a list of two-year degrees available from a local
community college in my area:

- Apprenticeship
- Architectural
- Carpentry

- Computer Information Systems
- Contract Education
- Construction Management
- Cosmetology
- Culinary Arts
- Electricity/Electronics Technology
- Engineering Technology
- Environmental Control
- Machine Technology
- Welding

Community colleges are popular because they're very inexpensive, local, and are often an excellent place to acquire vocational skills. For many, it serves as an alternative to the bachelor's degree in half the time and much less money. In the vocational areas, one can learn a trade and qualify for entry level positions in the workplace. Financial aid is available to those that qualify. An excellent resource for investigating colleges is www.petersons.com; at the website you can learn about costs, programs, resume writing, financial aid, test preparation and more. You can even apply online.

Bachelor's degree

Typically around 120-150 credits must be completed usually over a period of 4-5 years. A student takes a mixture of courses in the major, electives, and liberal arts. The breakdown if I remember correctly is usually something like:

- 45 % Liberal Arts
- 45% Courses in the major
- 10% Electives

When I received my Bachelor of Fine Arts degree I think that was the breakdown. The Bachelor of Arts (B.A.) and Bachelor of Science (B.S.) are the most common baccalaureates, and both include liberal arts courses, a major, and electives. The B.S. is more likely to be awarded in the sciences and for professional or technical fields of study. B.A. degrees are more often awarded in the humanities and arts. However, there are no absolute differences between the degrees, and policies concerning their award vary from college to college. Even if the bachelor's degree is not required for a particular position, in a tight labor market it certainly gives a competitive advantage.

> "Employers still prefer a four year college degree as preparation for information technology jobs. And in a tight job market, preference for a bachelor's degree rises as employers attempt to differentiate among potential job seekers." [14]

As competition in the workplace increases, it is hard to compete without a bachelor's degree. Ideally, it is best that you have already chosen what you wish to study before arriving at college. In general, college is not cheap. Those who have not decided what to study, or who change their major often, take longer to graduate, thus increasing the cost of their education.

When I attended college I don't recall any classes in how to choose a career; there certainly were no required courses. Everyone was expected to know what they wanted to study. There was a lot of pressure from peers and instructors to choose a major. Unfortunately, this pressure often causes students to hastily choose, or to continue in a major which may not have been the right one. Undergraduates are often under a great deal of pressure to choose their major, and to choose the right one. Sadly, our educational system does not require students to learn how to choose a career; nor the relationship between a major and a career.

Most of the occupational/technical skills that are learned at the undergraduate level could be taught in one year, or two at the most. Nonetheless, I believe the bachelor's degree is an excellent way of acquiring those transferable skills discussed earlier. The American population is becoming more educated, a bachelor's degree increasingly is a minimum qualification for employment. Despite this fact only about 25 percent of the U.S. population (over the age of 25) have bachelor's degrees.

> "HR executives ranked a traditional 4-year college degree in an IT-related field higher than an IT-industry-sponsored credential as the desired credential when considering hiring new employees."

An excellent resource for investigating colleges is www.petersons.com; at the website you can learn about costs, programs, resume writing, financial aid, test preparation and more. You can even apply online.

Degree Programs in Computing

There is a superb report titled "Computing Curricula 2004 Overview Report - A Guide to Undergraduate Degree Programs in Computing".[15] If you are seriously considering an undergraduate degree in computing it is worth reading. It goes into great detail in explaining the different undergraduate degree programs in the computing area. Not too long ago (10-15 years) all there was at the undergraduate level was the Bachelor of Science degree in Computer Science, today there are half a dozen. The number and types of degree programs are flourishing. Reading this report you will learn how academia is keeping up with the fast moving IT industry. It gives a superb breakdown of the skills developed and why they are important. A must read for anyone considering the study of computing, particularly at the undergraduate level. (It pays to be an educated consumer of education.) The report runs about 46 pages and is available free of charge on the internet. It can be found at www.ieee.org or www.acm.org. Below are excerpts from the report (italicized) describing five different undergraduate degrees available in computing.

Computer Engineering

Computer engineering is concerned with the design and construction of computers, and computer based systems. It involves the study of hardware, software, communications, and the interaction between them. Its curriculum focuses on the theories, principles, and practices of relevant areas of traditional electrical engineering and mathematics, and applies them to the problems of designing computers and the many kinds of computer-based devices.

Computer engineering students study the design of digital hardware systems, including computers, communications systems, and devices that contain computers. They also study software development with a focus on the software used within and between digital devices (not the software programs directly used by computer users). The emphasis of the curriculum is on hardware more than software, and it has a very strong engineering flavor.

Computer Science

Computer science spans a wide range, from its theoretical and algorithmic foundations to cutting-edge developments in robotics, computer vision, intelligent systems, bioinformatics, and other exciting areas. We can think of the work of computer scientists as falling into three categories:

• They develop effective ways to solve computing problems. For example, computer scientists develop the best possible ways to store information in databases, send data over networks, and display complex images. Their theoretical background allows

them to determine the best performance possible, and their study of algorithms lets them develop new problem-solving approaches that provide better performance.

• *They devise new ways to use computers. Progress in the CS areas of networking, database, and human-computer-interface came together as the world-wide-web, which changed the world. Now, researchers are working to make robots be practical aides and even demonstrate intelligence, databases create new knowledge and, in general, use computers to do new things.*

• *They design and implement software. Computer scientists take on challenging programming jobs. They also supervise other programmers, keeping them aware of new approaches.*

Computer science spans the range from theory to programming. Other disciplines can produce graduates better prepared for specific jobs, while computer science offers a comprehensive foundation that permits graduates to adapt to new technologies and new ideas.

Information Systems

Information systems specialists focus on integrating information technology solutions and business processes to meet the information needs of businesses and other organizations and enable organizations to achieve their objectives in an effective and efficient way. This discipline's perspective on "Information Technology" emphasizes information, and sees technology as an instrument to enable the generation, processing and distribution of needed information. Professionals in this discipline are primarily concerned with the information that computer systems can provide to aid the organization in defining and achieving its goals and the processes that organizations can implement using information technology. Information systems professionals often work in organizations that are large and complex, and with information systems that are correspondingly large and complex. They understand both technical and organizational factors, and must be able to help the organization determine how information and technology-enabled business processes can provide the organization with a competitive advantage.

The discipline now called information systems began more than forty years ago to address the data processing needs of business in the areas of accounting, payroll, and inventory. As the role of computing has expanded throughout the organization, so has the scope of information systems. Today, the information systems specialist plays a key role in determining the requirements for an organization's information systems and is active in their specification, design, and implementation. As a result, such professionals require a sound understanding of organizational principles and practices so that they can serve as an effective bridge between the technical and management communities within an organization, enabling them to work in harmony to ensure that the organization has the information and the systems it needs to support its operations. Information systems professionals are also involved in designing technology-based organizational communication and collaboration systems.

Most departments offering programs in Information Systems (IS) are located in business schools, and most IS degrees are combined computing and business degrees. A wide variety of IS programs exists under various labels which often reflect the nature of the program. For example, programs in Computer Information Systems usually have the strongest technology focus, whereas programs in Management Information Systems sometimes emphasize organizational and behavioral aspects of the IS discipline. The names of the degree programs are not consistent. Therefore, it is important to evaluate the details of the curriculum that a specific program follows to understand how its purpose.

Information Technology

Information technology is a label that has two meanings. In the broadest sense, we often use "information technology" interchangeably with "computer technology". In a more focused sense, it refers to academic degree programs that prepare students to meet the technology needs of business, government, healthcare, schools, and other kinds of organizations.

In the previous section, we said that the field of Information Systems focuses on the "information" aspects of "information technology". The field of Information Technology is the complement of that perspective. IT's emphasis is on the technology itself more than on the information it conveys. IT is a new and rapidly growing discipline, which started as a grass roots response to the practical, everyday needs of business and other organizations. Today, organizations of every kind are dependent on information technology. They need to have the appropriate systems in place. Those systems must work properly and be secure. Professionals must upgrade, maintain, and replace them as appropriate. The people who work throughout an organization require support from IT staff that thoroughly understands computer systems and are committed to solving whatever computer-related problems they might have. Graduates of information technology programs address these needs.

Degree programs in Information Technology arose because degree programs in the other computing disciplines failed to produce an adequate supply of graduates capable of handling these very real needs. IT programs exist to produce graduates who possess the right combination of knowledge and practical, hands-on expertise to take care of both an organization's information technology and the people who use it. IT specialists assume responsibility for selecting hardware and software products appropriate for an organization, integrating those products with organizational needs and infrastructure, and installing, customizing and maintaining those applications for the organization's computer users. Examples of these responsibilities include the installation of networks; network administration and security; the design of web pages; the development of multimedia resources; the installation of communication components; the oversight of email products; and the planning and management of the technology life-cycle by which an organization's technology is maintained, upgraded, and replaced.

Software Engineering

Software engineering is the discipline of developing and maintaining software systems that behave reliably and efficiently, and are affordable to develop and maintain. It has evolved in response to the increased importance of software in safety-critical applications and to the growing impact of large and expensive software systems in a wide range of situations. Traditionally, computer scientists produced software, and electrical engineers produced the hardware on which the software runs. As the size, complexity, and critical importance of software grew, so did the need to ensure that software performs as intended. By the early 1970s, it was apparent that proper software development practices require more than just the underlying principles of computer science; they also need the rigor that the engineering disciplines bring to the reliability and trustworthiness of the artifacts they engineer.

In the workplace, "software engineer" is a job label. There is no standard definition for this term when used in a job description. The role of a "software engineer" varies widely among employers. It can be a title equivalent to "computer programmer" or a title for someone who manages a large, complex, and/or safety-critical software project. The public must be mindful not confuse the discipline of software engineering with the ambiguous use of the term 'software engineer" as used in employment advertisements. The two terms often have very different meanings.

Master's degree

A master's degree is typically two-years, approximately 60 credits on average. I think it is one of the most effective degrees for developing skills for the workplace. The biggest advantage of a master's degree is -- that it means two-years of study exclusively in the area of choice. Generally, this means you're not spending any time taking liberal arts, or other unrelated classes. Like the bachelor's degree, the master's degree is nationally recognized, and the credits transferable. This means that if I complete half my coursework, and then decide to move to New York City, I can pick up where I left off, in another state. The credits are transferable. Nationally recognized means the degree that I'm awarded will be recognized in all 50 states, and many other countries.

> "By returning to graduate school and pursuing a Master's degree in instructional technology, I created an alternate career for myself as a computer trainer/instructor, as well as an IT support manager."
>
> - Lenny Bailes, Technical Writer & Instructor

I recommend master's degrees for anyone with a bachelor's, that wants to continue their education. A master's is also an excellent way for a working professional to make a career change. (In order to pursue a master's degree, one must have completed a bachelor's degree.) In 2-years one can acquire a professional degree and a new set of managerial or professional level skills. In the IT area there are a number of master's degrees offered; Master's of Business Administration/e-business, Master's of Science/CIS, for example. The teachers are often better, many are working professionals, and the degree is more focused on workplace skills. Master's degrees are also designed around working professionals and their busy schedules. Financial aid is available in most programs to those that qualify.

Certificates (non-credit)

Certificates have a unique place in the educational system, distinct from all the other educational offerings. Certificate programs are offered to the general public typically through colleges, universities, high schools, and private training outfits. Most certificates have no prerequisites and do not require completion of college, or sometimes even high school. First, the negatives about certificates: noncredit certificates for the most part are not transferable or nationally recognized. In other words, what is recognized in one state may not be recognized in another. Even within a state, a certificate offered by one School in C.I.S. may be completely different from the same certificate offered by another school. The certificates themselves are not accredited in any way, so there is no way to compare them with one another; for this reason they're not transferable. If you start a certificate program at one school it is best to finish it, because you will not be able to continue at another school in most cases.

Certificate programs have many advantages over the traditional bachelor's and master's degrees. The first advantage is time; certificate programs generally can be completed within one year, often within six months. They are designed with the working professional in mind, and therefore offer a convenient evening and weekend schedule in most cases. This can be a tremendous advantage for the working adult with a family. Depending on the nature and the number of instructional hours, certificate programs can cost anywhere from $500 to $5,000. Ironically, an advantage to certificate programs is the fact that they're not accredited. As a result, they do not have to go through the long, time consuming accreditation process. This means that certificate programs, generally have more current curricula. Any program of study offered within a bachelor's or master's degree must be accredited. Well-run certificate programs (as opposed to degrees) usually offer the latest technology, a flexible schedule, short duration, and instructors from the industry. In the area of Information Technology, learning the latest technology is critical. The better certificate programs are designed and run by (or with the guidance of) industry professionals as opposed to educators. Industry feedback can give a program more "real world" credibility. Just because an adult education program can be better designed (than an "academic" program) is no guarantee that it will be. Some adult education programs are well designed, taught by industry professionals, using the latest technology, others are not. Buyer beware.

Another advantage that certificate programs enjoy is their freedom to recruit faculty from the industry. Degree granting programs must use faculty that meet very high academic standards; typically a master's degree or a doctoral degree. Some industry professionals, even those at the highest levels, do not have these degrees, making them ineligible to teach at a university, even on a part time basis. (What this means is that some qualified professionals in the field, are often ineligible to teach in degree granting programs). This is a real drawback. Instructors with the latest industry knowledge are essential to offer the most current training in software and technology. One must hire those with the latest knowledge of what is used in today's workplace. Many university faculty have been on campus for years, teaching the same courses, they may be good teachers, but maybe their skill set is not up to date with the industry.

IT Industry certification (MCSE, CCNA)

Industry certification usually means a curriculum designed by a particular hardware or software manufacturer. For example, Microsoft is the creator of the very popular MCSE certification; Cisco is the creator of the very popular CCNA certification. Sometimes an industry group, or association such as CompTIA, will create a certification program such as A+ or Network+. According to Lenny Bailes "Many employers are now insisting on some computer certification as an entry-level requirement."

In general these types of certifications are an excellent way of getting your foot in the door for someone new to the field. Professionals who've been in the industry for many years often don't have, or need these certifications to gain employment. In my opinion they don't help as much for somebody who is already highly qualified, and has a proven employment track record. Some certification programs are better than others, if you're seriously considering the certification option, it would make sense to shop around before deciding on one. Certifications are sometimes requirements for a position, in which case you obviously must have the certification to qualify. Most knowledgeable employers do not require certifications, because having a certification should not be the sole measure of an applicants suitability. In the same way that a college degree in accounting is no guarantee that a graduate in accounting, is qualified for an entry level accounting position. Credentials or certifications are not guarantees of anything. My feeling is that they help those with minimal work experience the most. Certification does little to help a network administrator with ten years on the job, unless that person is acquiring new skills. That person has already proven their ability to do the job. (Certification can also help someone in the IT field already that wishes to move into a new area where they have no "on-the-job" experience.) Industry certification is usually obtained by taking and passing a test, or series of tests. At the moment Prometric is one of the larger testing organizations. Basically you go in and take a test (or tests) if you pass you are granted the certification or designation. You may study for the test (s) on your own using study guides, or you may take an exam preparation class. All the major IT book publishers (SYBEX, QUE, Thomson/Course Technology) have a selection of certification test preparation books. Web based certification training is also available.

How much education?

> "The discussion about career preparation for information technology occupations reveals that there is no universal education and training requirement for jobseekers in information technology. A computer-related degree may be the easiest and most direct route to take, but it is by no means the only one. There are a variety of ways in which workers can demonstrate the computer knowledge and skills necessary to get a job in one of several computer-related occupations." [16]

For the majority of Information Technology jobs a degree is not required to acquire the "skills" necessary for IT employment. I have found on occasion, highly qualified professionals without degrees. For most, due to the intense competition in the labor market, those without a degree are at a distinct disadvantage especially in a tight labor market, and "...according to the most extensive public opinion survey ever conducted about Americans' views on higher education '87% of Americans believe that a college education has become as important as a high school diploma used to be'" [17]

See page 113 for what the government believes the education requirements to be for some of the fastest growing occupations. I believe in general, the government overly emphasizes the need for degrees. The technical skills required for any of the positions mentioned -- could be acquired more rapidly in ways other than by completing a degree. As previously mentioned, a college education demonstrates to an employer much more than simply technical skill. It demonstrates commitment, determination, and a broad base of knowledge.

Basic literacy versus specialized skills

Ideally one has obtained basic literacy by the completion of high school. College then refines those skills and adds more. For an idea of what skills are developed in college see page 120. How does one determine the amount or type of specialized skills required for your career of choice? Let us suppose for example that you want to become a computer programmer. Computer programming is a large field and you will have to narrow it down to a particular language or languages. Let us suppose that the language C++ is very popular in the workplace, it actually is. Your research and industry contacts indicate this to be a wise choice. How well do you need to know C++ in order to get a job? Obviously, this depends on the job. You must do a little more research to find out what an entry level programmer must know. Speak to your industry contacts, or review the help wanted section of the newspaper. Another way of understanding what knowledge is required on the job, is to research the appropriate industry certification. These certifications were developed (usually by the industry) to address the employment needs of the industry. They "certify" that a person has a particular set of skills. These certifications can also give you an inside look at what skills are needed in your occupation of choice

Questions to ask yourself

- Do I possess basic literacy?
- Do I possess computer and information literacy?
- Can I speak clearly, and make myself understood on paper?
- What areas of my education need further refinement?
- Are my technical skills up to date?

Summary

- Your education should include the acquisition of basic literacy skills necessary to communicate orally and in writing
- Computer and information literacy are now a requirement to be an effective member of today's high-tech workforce
- Consider pursuing a degree or certificate to acquire relevant technical skills

SKILLS

Many people starting new careers mistakenly feel as though they have no skills; this is emphatically not the case. If you have not done so, take a moment to look at page 109. You will find that there are literally dozens of skills you probably already possess.

Erroneous Ideas about skills [18]

- People are not born with skills; all skills must be acquired
- Those skills which must be acquired, are acquired primarily in school environments
- If you have certain skills, you will be very aware that you have them
- Skills which are picked up in one field are only usable in that field; they are rarely transferable
- There are only a relatively few skills that individuals possess, none of which may turn out to be 'marketable'

How to get started developing IT skills

Presented below are some suggestions for how to get started acquiring IT skills; a recommended curriculum for those new to IT. If you have decided on a career in IT but are not sure where to start, these suggestions are for you. There are five subject areas that touch on all major occupational areas in IT. My recommendations are broad and general (and relate primarily to the PC platform) they provide the necessary foundation to pursue further study, or very entry-level employment in the IT industry.

Prerequisite knowledge for an IT career

- Basic Application software (Microsoft Office, Star Office, OpenOffice)
- Basic Operating Systems (Microsoft Windows, Linux, or UNIX)
- Basic PC Hardware troubleshooting and upgrading (CompTIA A+ certification)
- Basic Network Administration
- Basic Programming (Visual Basic, C++)

Basic knowledge of the above mentioned subjects typically will not be enough to land a job. One needs a more advanced set of skills. It is meant to give the reader a balanced set of introductory skills with which to pursue further study, or to help in choosing an area of specialization.

What skills are needed in IT?

You may be wondering what technical skills (or technologies) are utilized in the IT field. Which Operating Systems are typically used?; what should a Web Application Developer know? Below is a list that covers the major employment areas and the skills or technologies they utilize. The intent is to help the novice better understand the skill requirements. Keep in mind that technologies utilized in the IT field change rapidly. Regardless, the list should give you an idea of what occupations utilize which technologies or skills.

- PC Help Desk/User Support (skills in demand)
  Operating System software
  Application software
  Hardware
  Troubleshooting all of the above
- Database development (skills in demand)
  Oracle
  Sybase
  SAS
  Informix
  SQL/SQL server
- Programming (skills in demand)
  Visual Basic
  C++/Visual C++
  Java/JavaScript
  Pascal
  Microsoft .NET
- Web Application Development (skills in demand)
  Perl
  HTML
  Apache Web Server
  Internet Information Server
  Active Server Pages
  Extensible Markup Language (XML)
  Common Gateway Interface (CGI)
  Adobe Illustrator
  Macromedia Director
  Macromedia Dreamweaver
  Microsoft FrontPage
- Networking (skills in demand)
  Windows 2000
  Windows NT

Windows XP
Novell
Linux
Hardware knowledge
Operating system knowledge

When choosing a new career, do not over specialize
i.e. don't set your focus too narrowly when selecting a
career path. I know that this is easier said than done.
Most of us when we find what we want are eager to
jump right in. Your value in the workplace will be
greatly enhanced by having a broad base of skills at
least in the beginning. If you're too narrowly focused
on a particular technology or skill, your value to the
employer is limited. Resist the temptation to over
specialize in the beginning. Situations will arise in
the workplace requiring you to adapt, to adjust, to
learn new things. Having a good broad foundation, is
excellent preparation for the world of work ahead.
How one acquires the above mentioned skills depends
on many factors such as: what your current skill set
is? What area do you want to explore? How much
time do you have? How much money do you have?
For example: if you are a programmer already,
learning web application development is not such a
stretch. However, going from telecommunications to
programming, that is quite a stretch. If your
timeframe is short this represents another constraint.
For example, if you are already a programmer in
Oracle, learning Microsoft Access could be done in a
relatively short period of time. However, flirting with
a completely different specialization such as
telecommunications would take much longer. Below
are some ways to acquire IT skills.

Certification

In the world of IT industry certifications abound. A
few of the more popular ones are: Oracle, Microsoft,
Cisco, Red Hat, PeopleSoft, CompTIA, Solaris, and

Sun. There are at least a dozen well known certifications that I know of. Certification programs are excellent ways of acquiring skills for the workplace. Typically these programs are developed by industry professionals. If they're not developed by them they are at least developed in consultation with them. Such programs have a tangible "real world" component to them, as opposed to an academic thrust found in college and university environments. Typically, students prepare for certification by studying with a textbook; however today there are many on-line resources, as well as CBT's available. Some students prefer the classroom environment. To become certified one has to pass a test or tests. Regardless of how one prepares, industry certification is a viable way of acquiring skills, it also provides an entry level credential.

School

Most technologies are offered through traditional colleges and universities, if not, you may have to investigate private training organizations which are generally more expensive. Probably the best place to look would be in the adult education division of your local college, university, or high school. Adult education divisions typically offer the most cutting edge technology programs available to the general public.

Workplace

Most employers offer training to employees of some type, especially for employees in the Information Technology area. Because technology changes so rapidly training and re-training is a way of life. The advantage of workplace training is that the employer typically pays for it (and you get to spend some time away from the office!) Technology training in the workplace is often directly related to the work at hand. For example, if a new phone system is being installed, obviously the technical support staff need to be trained so they in turn can help others. Because IT training is expensive most employers limit it to the systems and applications they are currently working with. This can sometimes be a problem if the company is not using the latest technology. An employee can find themselves becoming less employable if their skill set is not current. At times it is necessary for IT workers to invest in their own education in order to stay current.

Self taught

> "I'm mostly self-taught. I've been lucky enough to establish writing contracts for books and magazine articles on operating systems and applications that have allowed me to experiment and be compensated for recording my experiences."
>
> - Lenny Bailes, Technical Writer & Instructor

Many IT professionals are self-taught. The IT field develops too quickly for colleges, universities, and book publishers to catch up. The web is often an essential resource for IT knowledge. One can find on-line articles, books, videos, and a whole host of learning resources.

> "Practice, practice, practice. Seriously, whenever I ran across an idea or technology I didn't know about, I read about it, asked someone, and/or read some code. If it looked interesting or relevant to what I was doing, I dug in and learned everything I could about it. Most people I know whose technical expertise I appreciate have taught themselves most of what they know. Doing so requires that the individual have a certain amount of curiosity and a lot of initiative. Technology changes

quickly, and technologists need to ride the wave."

- Philip Laird, Computer Scientist and Teacher

Volunteering/Internships

Being a volunteer is an excellent way of acquiring workplace skills that you can put on your resume. If you want to learn a particular technology; consider volunteering for a few hours per week with a professional who can teach you. This type of experience looks very attractive on a resume even though it is unpaid. Employers are less concerned with where you learned the skill; the important thing is that you have it. Any who are new to the IT field are faced with a dilemma; the fact that employers are not likely to hire you without experience. Volunteering is a way of developing a skill and experience at the same time. Volunteer opportunities are numerous, one way to find them is by using the internet. All the same can be said for Internships, which are typically found in schools or training programs.

Transferability of skills

Most skills are transferable, according to Richard N. Bowles 70% of our skills are transferable. This is a very interesting and important fact. In short, it means that the more you know about one thing, the easier it is to know about the next thing. If you know programming for example, learning web application development is that much easier. Many of the concepts are the same. The more you learn the easier it is to learn.

> "Many acquired skills are directly transferable to a new IT career. It is not just about tech skills."

- Mark Butler, Business Development Director,
Bay Area Technology Education Collaborative

How important are skills in the workplace?

So far I have not discussed "soft skills", in short the
ability to work successfully with others. What used to
be called "people skills". Working well with others is
critical in any occupation and should be taken
seriously by job applicants. If you are not able to
work well as part of a group your usefulness to an
organization is limited. 70% of CIO's said "soft
skills" were very important. See page 131.

Technical skills are also critical for employers. It is
very hard to be hired for any position unless you can
demonstrate that you possess the skills required.
How important are skills in the workplace? Very
important! At the beginning of this chapter I listed a
wide range of specialties in the IT area. In order for
you to have a chance of getting an interview with an
employer, you must demonstrate your proficiency in
one of those skills. Obviously, an employer is going
to give serious consideration to those that have used
the skill(s) at a previous employer. This demonstrates
that a candidate has work experience, and the skill in
question. For the hiring manager the best pick is
someone who has a combination of both skills and
experience.

Questions to ask yourself

- Have you chosen an area of specialization? If
  so, what skills are needed in the area you have
  chosen?
- If additional skills are needed, do you know
  where and how to acquire them?

Summary

- In order to work in the IT field one needs basic literacy, soft skills, and technical skills.
- There are many ways to acquire skills: on-the-job, school, self-taught, internships, etc.
- Determine for yourself which skills of yours need further honing or sharpening

E XPERIENCE

"Work experience is very important, but
it doesn't necessarily have to be paid for
it to prove valuable, especially for entry
level folks."

- Mark Butler, Business Development Director,
Bay Area Technology Education Collaborative

The benefits of work experience

Paid work experience is probably the most important
aspect of your resume to an employer. Most hiring
managers value work experience more than anything
else. First, it tells them that someone else hired you
and felt you were qualified for the job. For a hiring
manager extending an offer of employment involves
risk. The risk is that they might hire the wrong
person, thereby making the hiring manager look
incompetent. Or worse yet, hamper the productivity
of the department. When a hiring manager sees paid
work experience, it eliminates some of that risk. If
you've never been hired, it means no one has ever

taken a chance on you, and you remain unproven. The second thing that work experience gives the hiring manager is someone to call. Most employers expect that you would provide a reference for any significant employment experience you have had. As a result, the hiring manager could contact your former employer and ask about you. When the job market is tight, you can be certain the hiring manager will check your references. As a result, it is critical to develop and maintain a list of good references. An employee with work experience is regarded more highly than one without, in part because they can check your references, and see what kind of an employee you were. Obviously work experience is a tremendous asset to a job seeker.

If one does not have work experience the job seeker is at a distinct disadvantage, but all is not lost. If one does not have paid work experience one must highlight other aspects of the resume; maybe your skills or your education. Skills certainly are important to a hiring manager, as is education. Make the most of your education and skills, if experience is lacking. Consider working as an unpaid volunteer to develop experience.

When a job seeker has experience, obviously this is good. However there are different types of experience, relevant experience and irrelevant experience. Relevant experience is that which has a direct bearing on your ability to do the job in question. If one is applying for a computer job, relevant experience would be any programming experience. Irrelevant experience would be your summer vacation and how you spent it. Only highlight relevant experience on the resume. If you do not have relevant experience, you must somehow demonstrate aptitudes or skills you have that are relevant.

Experience on the resume is good but it must be relevant experience.

How do you get experience?

The age old conundrum, how do you get hired without experience? Entry-level job seekers have faced this problem since the beginning of time. Since experience is so important to employers, all jobseekers must face this issue at some point. There are many ways an inexperienced job seeker can beat the odds. One way is to have a genuine desire to help an organization. Having a genuine interest in an organization is one way to gain entry. If you are really interested in what they do, your excitement will show. Be persistent and enthusiastic, most organizations would welcome the help. If you are a student use that to your advantage, everyone likes to help a student. Ask for an internship through your school, invent one if you have to. Offer to go get coffee or donuts if they will allow you to do whatever it is you want to do. Where there is a will there is a way.

Working as an intern

> "Try to gain work experience with internships and volunteer labor. Look to non-profits to see if there is some short term project based work you can do in exchange for a reference."

> - Mark Butler, Business Development Director, Bay Area Technology Education Collaborative

Volunteering

Working as a volunteer is an excellent way of developing experience, albeit unpaid. Volunteer work has all the benefits of "real" work except the money. From the hiring managers point of view it is not quite as good as "real" experience but is often not far behind. Let's consider an example of two candidates that are applying for an entry-level Personal

Computer Technical Support position. Each candidate has recently completed a training program in Personal Computer Technical Support. Candidate A in addition to the training has completed a six-month Internship at a local computer store and has a glowing reference from his boss. Which candidate do you feel has the better shot?

Questions to ask yourself

- Do I have enough relevant work experience?
- Have I investigated internship or volunteer opportunities?

Summary

- Work experience is very important on the resume
- develop a plan to make sure that you have relevant work experience

HOW TO FIND AN IT JOB

"The best way is to ask people you know in the industry ("networking"). Recruiters have their value, but the job seeker should remember that recruiters are paid by the employers, not the employee. Unpaid internships are sometimes available, especially through non-profits and technical training programs; they put invaluable expertise on the resume..."

- Philip Laird, Computer Scientist and Teacher

Decide what it is you would like to do

The next step is to decide what kind of a job you would like within an organization. Sometimes the two steps are done simultaneously. For example, if I want to be a teacher, it's obvious that I would look to schools for work. In this case the organization and the job are closely linked to. Sometimes the link between organization and job is not so clear, take Certified Public Accountants (CPA) for example. A CPA can be self employed, or work for a non-profit, a school, or a bank. Almost all organizations need accountants, the government, nonprofits, commercial banks, insurance companies, and a whole host of other large and small organizations. Deciding what you would like to do within an organization helps you to focus. Once you know what you want to do, you will then know how to track down the person doing the hiring. (It is critical to know what you want to do at this point.) For example, if I want to be a computer programmer in the banking industry, I would contact the M. I. S. department at local banks. Focusing your job search is essential; you cannot be effective until you decide what you are looking for and where.

Select a group of organizations

Start by choosing organizations consistent with your values and interests. Are you interested in working for a large or small company, a non-profit or for profit? Many of us when job hunting target the whole world out of desperation or ignorance. The first step in finding a job is to narrow the field. It is impossible to focus if you are targeting everything. At this point you should have some skills and experience to offer an employer. Now you must decide what type of organization you would like to work for. Learn as much as possible about the organization in order to make yourself a better candidate. What is their business? How are they doing? Are they facing layoffs? Your value to the organization will depend on your ability to understand their needs. The type of organization you are pursuing, and the job you want, will dictate how to prepare your resume and cover letter. The scattershot approach does not work because each organization is different. Applying for a job at an educational institution is very different from applying for a job at a bank, or a financial institution. When looking for a job it is important to have an understanding not only of the job, but the organization.

> "Read the job listings on web-based employment services. Volunteer as an intern, if you can't immediately find a paying job. Check into the situation with schools and nonprofit companies in your area to see whether they're looking for volunteer help."
>
> - Lenny Bailes, Technical Writer & Instructor

Making a list of organizations you're interested in helps narrow the field and makes your task manageable. Focusing your efforts will improve your effectiveness. It is simply not possible to pursue all jobs in all organizations, you must be selective. Your selection criteria should be created by you based on your priorities. For example, one of my criteria was that my job needed to be in the same city where I live. Another criteria for me was that the job needed to be with an organization involved in IT training. These criteria though few, enabled me to pursue an effective job search strategy. It significantly narrowed the prospects, and allowed me to quickly focus only on organizations that met my needs.

Most Effective Methods of Job Hunting [19]

According to Richard Nelson Bolles the most effective methods of finding a job are:
- Asking for job leads from family, friends, the community
- Going door to door
- Using the phone

Least Effective methods of Job Hunting [20]

- Using the Internet
- Mailing out resumes to employers at random
- Answering ads in newspapers, trade journals etc

There is an often heard phrase in the job hunting world "the hidden job market". It refers to all the jobs that are never posted. It is commonly held that the most effective ways of job hunting allow you to tap into the "hidden job market". Based on the above my recommended job search strategy is the following:

- Target a group of organizations you would like to work for
- Determine what department and person could use your help
- Learn what this person wants and needs
- Arrange a meeting to discuss how you can help them and vice versa
- Ask if you may keep in touch periodically
- Ask if there is anyone else you should contact

Find the person that can hire you

After you've decided on an organization and the type of work you would like to do, you must now find the person that can hire you. Many organizations will try and prevent job seekers from finding the hiring manager. It is important to realize that companies are inundated with job seekers trying to get interviews. If you're having difficulty contacting the hiring manager, try contacting the department or division, do not mention that you are a job seeker. Try and use the company's website to locate the hiring manager. With a little determination you will locate the proper person, but it might take a little effort. Another way to get to the hiring manager is to ask for a meeting to discuss the industry. Most managers love to talk shop. Take advantage of this fact. When requesting such a meeting simply say that you're considering beginning a career in that field and want to get more information. Ask for an informational interview. Before contacting this person you want to make sure you have an understanding of the business, and the position you are interested in. Come prepared if you want to make a good impression.

One of the most effective ways to find the hiring manager is to find out if any of your friends or family, work for the organization in question. If so, it will be very easy to find the hiring manager. Not only can they lead you to the hiring manager, they can also give you inside information about the company. For example, how the company is doing financially? Are they experiencing layoffs? If an acquaintance of yours knows the hiring manager they may be able to intercede on your behalf and arrange a meeting or interview, and possibly serve as a reference for you. Personal contacts can be critical to helping you find a job. We've all heard the expression it's "who you know", and this is very true. Using your own personal network is probably one of your best sources for job leads, because it is personal and direct. Be sure to have a personal network. Tell your friends and family that you're looking for work, and tell them what kind of work your looking for.

> "Don't overlook staffing and outsource firms. They may have few entry level positions, but in our experience they do get call- outs for less experienced folks, and tend not to actively recruit these people for their employee pool. By having a resume on file, and periodically checking in you may find yourself in the right place at the right time."
>
> - Mark Butler, Business Development Director, Bay Area Technology Education Collaborative

Request an interview

Once you find the person with the power to hire, it is critical that you make a good first impression. You must be dressed appropriately, be knowledgeable of their line of business, and have a goal in mind. Do not waste this person's time. If you're not ready to look for a job, use this opportunity to conduct what is called an informational interview. An informational interview is an interview where your objective is to gather information, as opposed to a job offer. An informational interview can be used for any of the following reasons:

- To develop industry contacts
- To find out about a particular company
- To find out about a particular occupation
- To find out about internship or volunteer opportunities

This is an interview where you're seeking information as opposed to a job. It is a wonderful way of finding out more about the company, or more about the line of work. It is particularly beneficial for those looking to start a new career. It is a stress-free conversation for both parties, because there's no pressure of the job offer. The hiring manager will feel relieved and so will you, because you're not looking for a job. An informational interview can be an excellent way to learn about a particular occupation or organization. For example, suppose I am a web application developer, and I'm considering becoming a network administrator. Conducting informational interviews can help me understand what the life of a network administrator is like. What are the challenges that network administrators face? What kind of training do they have? What are the salaries like? I have used informational interviews myself and have found them very effective.

Charm/Personality

Be a likable person. I know it sounds silly but people want to be around people they like. Everyone likes a charming personality, someone that is comfortable around others, someone that works well with others. Someone that is likable. Everyone wants likable people in their organization. Many jobseekers do not realize this fact. It should not simply be an act, being likable is very important. It is particularly important for the hiring manager to like you.

Persistence/Determination

As with anything good in life, persistence is often required to achieve it. Everyone knows of good ideas that were never pursued. Without persistence and follow-up even the best ideas will never be realized. If you're interested in pursuing a particular job (or career) you must be willing to persist. Your persistence will not be lost on the hiring manager. If the hiring manager sees that you are persistent it helps them to evaluate you in a positive light. Especially since persistence & determination are desirable traits for an employee to have. Use this fact to your advantage.

The power of networking

I was attending a conference on e-Government. I saw that there would be an interesting panel discussion taking place and decided to attend. The topic of the panel was how city government was changing as a result of technology and the internet. As I was waiting for them to begin I recognized the Chair of the panel from a photograph. I decided to introduce myself, it couldn't hurt. After telling him what I do, he became very excited and asked if I would like to join the panel. Stunned, I accepted and joined the panel. After the panel was over I shook hands with and chit-chatted with a number of esteemed professionals, leaders in my field. While leaving the conference I was on cloud nine, I was a panelist; I was videotaped and got to meet some big shots. End of story? Not yet. A few years later, I saw a job

opening I was interested in. I went down to the
organization to find out more, and maybe speak with
the Chief Information Officer (CIO). When I arrived,
I had a chance to speak with his assistant. As I was
leaving, in walked the CIO. We stared at each other
speechless for a few moments. We then recognized
each other as both having participated on the e-
Government panel. We then engaged in a few minutes
of "small world" chit-chat, he then asked why I was at
his office. I told him I was interested in the job
opening in his department. We talked for about half
an hour about the position, he then introduced me to
his staff. He offered me the job "on the spot" no
resume, no application, nothing! Needless to say I was
stunned! This had never happened to me before, and
it may never happen again, but it taught me one thing.
Networking works! The more people you know in
your line of work, the better. Get out and meet
people, especially people that can hire you.

Develop industry contacts

It is essential for job seekers to develop industry
contacts. In order to understand the industry, it is
very important to talk with those who are in it.
Because a newcomer to the field knows so little about
the industry, it is even more important to seek the
council of industry professionals. Despite the
importance of developing these types of contacts,
very few career changers actually do. It is important
to develop industry contacts for the following
reasons:

- To see if you like the work
- To find out information about salaries
- To help choose an area of specialization
- To find out what skills are required
- To obtain job hunting advice
- To find out which companies are hiring

- To get help developing your resume

My suggestion is that you develop a half dozen industry contacts, to help inform you about your career choice. Initially, they can help you to decide what area of IT you may want to pursue. If you're considering a career as a programmer it might be helpful to have a career contact that is a programmer. If you're considering a career as a network administrator it might also be helpful to have a career contact that is a network administrator. Use your career contacts to help you select (or learn about) an area of specialization. Visit the workplace and see what "a-day-in-the-life" is like.

Your industry contacts can also help you find a job. As your career progresses you'll be developing new skills. By keeping in touch with your career contacts they can make you aware of job opportunities that you qualify for. This is an excellent way of getting your first, second, or third job, through personal contacts. We have all heard the expression "it's not what you know, it's who you know". Personal contact (also known as networking) is one of the most effective means of getting a job. Keeping in contact with your career contacts over the years will greatly increase the effectiveness of your job searches.

Online Job Searching

The computerization of the job search function provides tremendous benefits. Today one can search thousands of job listings in seconds with the click of a mouse. One can look for a job out of town just as quickly as looking locally. The conglomeration of a large number of jobs in one place (searchable by the user) makes it a very effective tool.

As with many other contemporary tasks, job searching has become automated. The job search today would not be complete without making use of the internet. In order to make use of these tools one must be familiar with how to use the internet, and how to access web pages. If you're not familiar with these tasks I would suggest taking a class on how to use the internet. The websites that I use, and am most familiar with are: www.hotjobs.com and www.monster.com, there are many others. For those not familiar with these, they are web sites that allow you to post your resume and search for jobs. Employers can find your resume, and you can find job openings listed by many employers. It is often free to list your resume and to search for jobs; however employers must pay to list their jobs. There are websites that specialize in government jobs, nonprofit jobs, education jobs, and computer jobs. It is worth investigating the different websites to find the most effective ones to aid you in your job search. Below are some of the more popular ones:

- www.monster.com
- www.hotjobs.com
- www.craigslist.org
- www.usajobs.com (government jobs)
- www.dice.com (computer jobs)
- http://chronicle.com/jobs (education jobs)

Effectiveness

In order to use the websites effectively one must understand their limitations. One is that not all employers can afford to post their jobs online. Like everything else this costs money. Most employers today have web sites that list their own job openings. Many jobs are not advertised on the big sites mentioned above, because the employer lists them on their own site. You may see a job posted by a particular employer one month and not the next. Many employers use the service sparingly due to cost.

Don't be under the mistaken assumption that all
employers list their jobs on www.monster.com or
www.hotjobs.com, or any other site for that matter.
The second reason why many online job searches are
not effective is that most people don't use the
websites effectively. For those with little experience
working with databases I recommend taking a basic
database search class, many libraries offer them for
free. Or, just read up on the topic on the internet, or
check out a book from the library. Online searching
or database searching is not a complex topic at the
user level. A database is only effective if one knows
how to search it effectively. Making this task more
difficult is that each database is different. One must
spend time getting to know how each database works,
in order to use it effectively.

Suggestions

- Include searchable keywords on your resume
- Post your resume online at one or more sites
- Work with a selected site until you understand
  how it works, and how to get the best results
- Find out which employers you are interested in
  and check their websites as well
- Apply for jobs you are interested in online, but
  follow-up through more conventional means
  (mail, telephone, networking)
- Utilize saved searches, many of the job sites
  allow you to save the criteria you created

Limitations

The online job search is an excellent way to quickly
develop job leads for you to pursue. Many job seekers
are under the mistaken impression that everything can
be done online; everything from finding the job, to
applying for the job, to getting the job offer. First,
employers never make hiring decisions based on what

is on a computer screen. A realistic expectation is that you can use the online job search to find job leads, with which to pursue. The pursuit of those leads might be by mail, in person, or on the phone, or through networking. Don't see the computer as the total solution, this is an unrealistic expectation. The online job search should only be part of your repertoire. It should give you some sense of what is available in your area, and provide you with viable job leads for you to pursue. Keep in mind that one of the drawbacks is you're competing with all the other people that saw the job opening. In this respect it has the same drawbacks that a newspaper advertisement does, all the other applicants you're competing against. Be sure that your job search strategy includes: networking, telephone calling, meeting employers face to face, in addition to the online searching component.

Searching

In addition to posting your resume you may also configure "saved searches" to facilitate your search. The "saved search" allows you to establish a criteria in order to filter out the many jobs which don't meet the criteria. Because the search criteria are saved, you can use them repeatedly. You can even have the results of the search sent to you in email. For example, if I live in New York City I may want to select jobs that are near my home. In this case one of my criteria would be location. Other criteria would typically be the job title, for example "Computer Programmer". With just these two criteria I can significantly reduce the number of useless job leads. Quite often the problem is too much information, as opposed to too little. One needs to learn how to limit the number of jobs, and focus on those of most interest. Because each search engine is different, this is not an easy task. One must spend time working with each search engine and experiment with the different parameters. For example, in www.hotjobs.com there are about thirty different categories of jobs, however you can only select three in your job search. In effect this means for each "saved search" that you create, you're only searching 1/10 of the database. As a result, it makes sense to periodically change your categories so that over time you have searched all job categories. Each website is different, experiment until you are getting a satisfactory selection of jobs that interest you.

The Electronic Resume

Today large employers and placement agencies are scanning most resumes electronically. In effect they are creating their own databases. This means that your beautifully prepared and formatted resume is being broken into bits and bytes to be searched by the computer. All kidding aside this is a good thing, because it means more employers can find you quickly. All one needs to do is include a section in their resume called "KEY WORDS". In this section list the key functions, skills, or responsibilities that you possess. What you're trying to achieve is as clear a picture what the employer is looking for. You want to get into the mind of the employer as best you can. To do this you must know the key words that the employer will use when scanning the resume database. Is education or certification important? Should they be included in your key words? Are your skills important? In much the same way job seekers search for employers online; employers search for employees online in the same way using key words.

It is beyond the scope of this book to include a section on resume preparation. I do recommend two excellent books on the subjects of resumes [21] and cover letter preparation.[22] The author Richard Beatty suggests there are eight "knockout" factors that employment managers use when reviewing and eliminating resumes; they are:

- Job objective incompatible with current openings
- Inappropriate or insufficient educational credentials
- Incompatible salary requirements
- Geographic restrictions incompatible with current openings
- Lack of U.S. citizenship or permanent resident status
- Resume poorly organized, sloppy, or hard to read
- Too many employers in too short a period of time
- Too many pages – a book instead of a resume

When preparing your resume keep these "knockout" factors in mind.

Questions to ask yourself

- Where do you want to work and what do you want to do?
- Have you prepared your resume and cover letter?
- Have you put your resume online?

Summary

- Develop a plan for which organizations you would like to approach
- Decide what you want to do for these organizations
- Prepare a resume and cover letter, keep in mind the knockout factors above

- Develop a unique resume and cover letter for each job
- Find the person that can hire you
- Be persistent
- Develop industry contacts
- Post your resume online and use keywords so it can be searched
- Create a list of web sites to check periodically for job openings

C HARTS AND TABLES
TABLE 1: SELF ASSESSMENT – STEP 1

Your field or occupation		
List each "Field" (or Occupation) you have worked in related to your current career. Make the grid fit your life, add more columns or rows as needed. Examples of three fields are provided: Programmer, Trainer, Help Desk.		
Field 1:	Field 2:	Field 3:
Programmer	IT Trainer	Help Desk

TABLE 2: SELF ASSESSMENT – STEP 2

Your job titles in each field or occupation
The purpose of this worksheet is to jog your memory. Many of us have had jobs we don't even remember. It helps to list all your titles in your various careers or fields. List in any order. Doing this will help prepare you for step 3. See examples below.

Field 1. Programmer	Field 2. IT Trainer	Field 3. Help Desk
Title 1. Systems Analyst	Title 1. Adjunct Lecturer	Title 1. IS Administrator
Title 2. Programmer I	Title 2. Trainer	Title 2. PC Support
Title 3. IS Analyst	Title 3. Instructor	Title 3. Help Desk
Title 4. Developer	Title 4. Program Director	Title 4. Support Analyst
Title 5.	Title 5.	Title 5.
Title 6.	Title 6.	Title 6.
Hobby 1.	Hobby 1.	Hobby 1.

TABLE 3: SELF ASSESSMENT – STEP 3

Favorite skills acquired in each field or occupation		
List six favorite skills developed in each field, in ascending order "most" favorite to "least" favorite. See examples below.		
Field 1. Programmer	Field 2. IT Trainer	Field 3. Help Desk
Skill 1. Analyzing	Skill 1. Mentoring	Skill 1. Troubleshooting
Skill 2. Checking	Skill 2. Teaching	Skill 2. Fixing
Skill 3. Programming	Skill 3. Communicating	Skill 3. Analyzing
Skill 4. Diagnosing	Skill 4. Preparing	Skill 4. Diagnosing
Skill 5. Problem solving	Skill 5. Supervising	Skill 5. Installing
Skill 6. Organizing	Skill 6. Designing	Skill 6. Helping

TABLE 4: SELF ASSESSMENT – STEP 4

Favorite skills acquired in all fields & occupations RELATED TO PEOPLE List your six favorite skills or activities related to people. Rather than using one word verbs as in STEP 3, here you can flesh it out. You may use skills from STEP 3 but make them more specific and particular. You may also add new skills not found in STEP 3. List in ascending order "most" favorite to "least" favorite. See examples below.
Skills or Activities
1. Mentoring, students that I teach helping them make career decisions
2. Teaching, in a classroom setting
3. Helping, people with their computer problems
4.
5.
6.

TABLE 5: SELF ASSESSMENT – STEP 5

Favorite skills acquired in all fields & occupations RELATED TO DATA List your six favorite skills related to data. Rather than using one word verbs as in STEP 3, here you can flesh it out. You may use skills from STEP 3 but make them more specific and particular, see the example. You may also add new skills not found in STEP 3. List in ascending order "most" favorite to "least" favorite. See examples below.
Skills or Activities
1. Problem solving, while working on a computer program
2. Preparing, a lesson plan to teach a class
3. Designing, IT curricula and training programs
4.
5.
6.

TABLE 6: SELF ASSESSMENT – STEP 6

Favorite skills acquired in all Fields & Occupations
RELATED TO THINGS
List your six favorite skills related to things. Rather than using one word verbs as in STEP 3, here you can flesh it out. You may use skills from STEP 3 but make them more specific and particular, see example. You may also add new skills not found in STEP 3. List in ascending order "most" favorite to "least" favorite.
Skills or Activities
1. Troubleshooting, computer & network hardware to make it perform properly
2. Fixing, hardware or software problems
3.
4.
5.
6.

TABLE 7: SELF ASSESSMENT – STEP 7

Favorite Skills and how you like to use them Here is where you compile a master list of your favorite skills taken from STEPS 4-6. If your favorite skill is working with PEOPLE choose item # 1 from STEP 4 and put it first. If the skills you most prefer using are related to DATA, select item #1 from STEP 5. If the skills you most prefer using are related to THINGS select item # 1 from STEP 6. List in ascending order "most" favorite to "least" favorite. Fill-in as many blanks as you can. If all your favorite skills are used with people, no problem.
Skills or Activities
1. Mentoring, students that I teach helping them make career decisions
2. Problem solving, while writing computer programs
3.
4.
5.
6.

TABLE 8: SELF ASSESSMENT

Occupation and field - examples	
Identify your current occupation and field. See examples below. Doing this will help you see the relationship between occupation and field. It may give you some ideas.	
Occupation-What you do	Field/Industry-Where you do it
Teacher	Education
Nurse	Health Care
Program Manager	Construction
Scientist	Agriculture
Accountant	Financial services
Lawyer	Health care
Consultant	Music, recording industry

TABLE 9: SELF ASSESSMENT

Where are you now? (Fill in the blanks) See where you are and get some ideas of where you might want to go.	
Occupation-what you do now	Field/Industry-Where you do it

Where do you want to be? (Fill in the blanks) See where you may want to go.	
Occupation-what you want to do	Field/Industry-Where you want to do it

TABLE 10: LIST OF TRANSFERABLE SKILLS

<u>**achieving**</u>
acting
adapting
addressing
administering
advising
analyzing
anticipating
arbitrating
arranging
ascertaining
assembling
assessing
attaining
auditing
<u>**budgeting**</u>
building
calculating
<u>**charting**</u>
checking
classifying
coaching
collecting
communicating
compiling
completing
composing
computing
conceptualizing
conducting
conserving
consolidating
constructing
controlling
coordinating
coping

counseling
creating
<u>**deciding**</u>
defining
delivering
designing
detailing
detecting
determining
developing
devising
diagnosing
digging
directing
discovering
dispensing
displaying
disproving
dissecting
distributing
diverting
dramatizing
drawing
driving
<u>**editing**</u>
eliminating
empathizing
enforcing
establishing
estimating
evaluating
examining
expanding
experimenting
explaining
expressing

extracting
filing
financing
fixing
following
formulating
founding
gathering
generating
getting
giving
guiding
handling
harnessing
heading
helping
humanizing
hypothesizing
identifying
illustrating
imagining
implementing
improving
improvising
increasing
influencing
informing
initiating
innovating
inspecting
inspiring
installing
instituting
instructing
integrating
interpreting
interviewing
intuiting

inventing
inventorying
investigating
joking
jousting
judging
juggling
justifying
keeping
knowing
leading
learning
lecturing
lifting
listening
logging
maintaining
making
managing
manipulating
mediating
meeting
memorizing
mentoring
modeling
monitoring
motivating
naming
navigating
negotiating
networking
nursing
observing
obtaining
offering
operating
ordering
organizing

originating
overseeing
painting
perceiving
performing
persuading
piloting
planning
playing
predicting
preparing
prescribing
presenting
printing
problem solving
processing
producing
programming
projecting
promoting
proof-reading
protecting
providing
publicizing
purchasing
quelling
questioning
raising
reading
realizing
reasoning
receiving
recommending
reconciling
recording
recruiting
reducing
referring

rehabilitating
relating
remembering
rendering
repairing
reporting
representing
researching
resolving
responding
restoring
retrieving
reviewing
risking
scheduling
selecting
selling
sensing
separating
serving
setting
setting-up
sewing
shaping
sharing
showing
singing
sketching
solving
sorting
speaking
studying
summarizing
supervising
supplying
symbolizing
synergizing
synthesizing

systematizing
talking
teaching
team-building
telling
tending
testing
training
transcribing
translating
traveling
trouble-shooting
tutoring

typing
umpiring
understanding
understudying
undertaking
unifying
upgrading
utilizing
verbalizing
weighing
winning
working
writing

TABLE 11: FASTEST GROWING OCCUPATIONS [23]

Fastest growing occupations and occupations projected to have the largest numerical increases in employment between 2002 and 2012, by level of education or training	
Fastest growing occupations	**Occupations having the largest numerical job growth**
First professional degree	
1. Pharmacists	Lawyers
2. Veterinarians	Physicians and surgeons
3. Chiropractors	Pharmacists
4. Physicians and surgeons	Clergy
5. Optometrists	Veterinarians
Doctoral degree	
1. Postsecondary teachers	Postsecondary teachers
2. Computer and information scientists, research	Clinical, counseling, and school psychologists
3. Medical scientists, except epidemiologists	Medical scientists, except epidemiologists
4. Clinical, counseling, and school psychologists	Computer and information scientists, research
5. Biochemists and biophysicists	Biochemists and biophysicists
Master's degree	
1. Physical therapists	Physical therapists
2. Mental health and substance abuse social workers	Rehabilitation counselors
3. Rehabilitation counselors	Educational, vocational, and school counselors
4. Survey researchers	Mental health and substance abuse social workers
5. Epidemiologists	Market research analysts
Bachelor's or higher degree, plus work experience	

Fastest growing occupations and occupations projected to have the largest numerical increases in employment between 2002 and 2012, by level of education or training

	Fastest growing occupations	Occupations having the largest numerical job growth
1.	Computer and information systems managers	General and operations managers
2.	Education administrators, preschool and childcare center/program	Management analysts
3.	Sales managers	Financial managers
4.	Management analysts	Sales managers
5.	Medical and health services managers	Computer and information systems managers
Bachelor's degree		
1.	Network systems and data communications analysts	Elementary school teachers, except special education
2.	Physician assistants	Accountants and auditors
3.	Computer software engineers, applications	Computer systems analysts
4.	Computer software engineers, systems software	Secondary school teachers, except special and vocational education
5.	Database administrators	Computer software engineers, applications
Associate degree		
1.	Medical records and health information technicians	Registered nurses
2.	Physical therapist assistants	Computer support specialists
3.	Veterinary technologists and technicians	Medical records and health information technicians
4.	Dental hygienists	Dental hygienists
5.	Occupational therapist assistants	Paralegals and legal assistants
Postsecondary vocational award		

Fastest growing occupations and occupations projected to have the largest numerical increases in employment between 2002 and 2012, by level of education or training

	Fastest growing occupations	Occupations having the largest numerical job growth
1.	Fitness trainers and aerobics instructors	Preschool teachers, except special education
2.	Preschool teachers, except special education	Licensed practical and licensed vocational nurses
3.	Respiratory therapy technicians	Automotive service technicians and mechanics
4.	Emergency medical technicians and paramedics	Hairdressers, hairstylists, and cosmetologists
5.	Security and fire alarm systems installers	Fitness trainers and aerobics instructors
Work experience in a related occupation		
1.	Self-enrichment education teachers	First-line supervisors/managers of retail sales workers
2.	Emergency management specialists	First-line supervisors/managers of food preparation and serving workers
3.	Private detectives and investigators	First-line supervisors/managers of office and administrative support workers
4.	First-line supervisors/managers of protective service workers, except police, fire, and corrections	First-line supervisors/managers of construction trades and extraction workers
5.	Detectives and criminal investigators	Self-enrichment education teachers
Long-term on-the-job training		
1.	Heating, air-conditioning, and refrigeration mechanics	Electricians

Fastest growing occupations and occupations projected to have the largest numerical increases in employment between 2002 and 2012, by level of education or training

	Fastest growing occupations	Occupations having the largest numerical job growth
	and installers	
2.	Audio and video equipment technicians	Police and sheriff's patrol officers
3.	Tile and marble setters	Carpenters
4.	Police and sheriff's patrol officers	Cooks, restaurant
5.	Electricians	Plumbers, pipefitters, and steamfitters
Moderate-term on-the-job training		
1.	Medical assistants	Customer service representatives
2.	Social and human service assistants	Truck drivers, heavy and tractor-trailer
3.	Hazardous materials removal workers	Sales representatives, wholesale and manufacturing, except technical and scientific products
4.	Dental assistants	Medical assistants
5.	Residential advisors	Maintenance and repair workers, general
Short-term on-the-job training		
1.	Home health aides	Retail salespersons
2.	Physical therapist aides	Combined food preparation and serving workers, including fast food
3.	Occupational therapist aides	Cashiers, except gaming
4.	Personal and home care aides	Janitors and cleaners, except maids and housekeeping cleaners
5.	Security guards	Waiters and waitresses

Source: *U.S. Department of Labor, Bureau of Labor Statistics*, Bulletin 2540, Occupational Outlook Handbook. 2/27/2004.

TABLE 12: IMPORTANCE OF QUALIFICATIONS[24]

Desired qualifications of non-managerial IT applicants

Type of qualification	Percentage of respondents
High-school diploma	97.0
2-year college degree	71.0
4-year degree in IT-related field	63.6
4-year degree in non-IT-related field	25.0
Master's degree in IT-related field	15.6
Master's degree in non-IT-related field	3.2
IT-industry-sponsored credentials	62.5

HR executives were asked to indicate the type of qualifications they would like in applicants for IT jobs. Respondents indicated the qualification/degree was either "important" or "very important".

Source: Bartlett, Kenneth "The Perceived Influence of Industry-Sponsored Credentials". University of Minnesota, Copyright 2002. Reprinted with permission: *National Research Center for Career and Technical Education, University of Minnesota, St. Paul, MN*, The National Dissemination Center for Career and Technical Education, Ohio State University, Columbus, OH (page 48).

TABLE 13: HIGHEST LEVEL OF EDUCATION
25

(IT Employees)

Credentials	Percentage
High School	5.3
Some College or Formal Training	38.4
2-year Associate's Degree	22.0
4-year College Degree	25.3
Master's Degree or above	8.6
Missing	1.4

Total   **100.0**

Source: Bartlett, Kenneth "The Perceived Influence of Industry-Sponsored Credentials". University of Minnesota, Copyright 2002. Reprinted with permission: *National Research Center for Career and Technical Education, University of Minnesota, St. Paul, MN,* The National Dissemination Center for Career and Technical Education, Ohio State University, Columbus, OH (page 57).

TABLE 14: SKILLS ACQUIRED IN COLLEGE

In 1975 while at San Francisco State University, Paul Breen and Urban Whitaker prepared a report documenting the skills acquired via an undergraduate education in the liberal arts. In consultation with employers, students, and faculty, they developed a comprehensive list, divided into nine groupings of skills. The skills are thought to be "generally recognized as essential in a variety of careers and other activities." Although some of the skills may seem so simple, or so fundamental as to not be worth articulating, this is emphatically not the case. They are indeed sophisticated capabilities that not everyone possesses. Your readiness to discuss confidently and concretely your possession of these skills, and others, will prove invaluable when you begin presenting yourself to potential employers.

- **Information and Management Skills**
  - o Sort data and objects
  - o Compile and rank information
  - o Apply information creatively to specific problems or tasks
  - o Synthesize facts, concepts and principles
  - o Understand and use organizing principles
  - o Evaluate information according to appropriate standards

- **Design and Planning Skills**
    - Identify alternative courses of action
    - Set realistic goals
    - Follow through with a plan or decision
    - Manage time effectively
    - Predict future trends and patterns
    - Accommodate multiple demands for commitment of time, energy, and resources
    - Assess needs
    - Make and keep a schedule
    - Set priorities

- **Research and Investigative Skills**
  - Use a variety of sources of information
  - Apply a variety of methods to test the validity of data
  - Identify problems and needs
  - Design an experiment, plan or model to define a problem systematically
  - Identify informational sources appropriate to special needs or problems
  - Formulate relevant questions to clarify a problem, topic or issue
- **Communication Skills**
  - Listen with objectivity and paraphrase with accuracy
  - Use various writing styles and forms
  - Speak effectively to individuals and groups
  - Use media to present ideas imaginatively
  - Express one's needs, wants, opinions and preferences without violating the rights of others
  - Identify and effectively express value judgments
  - Describe objects or events with few factual errors
  - Convey a positive self-image

- **Human Relations and Interpersonal Skills**
  - Keep a group moving toward the achievement of a common goal
  - Maintain group cooperation and support
  - Delegate tasks and responsibilities
  - Interact effectively with peers, superiors and subordinates
  - Express one's feelings appropriately
  - Understand the feelings of others
  - Persuade and argue well
  - Make commitments
  - Be willing to take risks
  - Teach a skill, concept or principle to others
  - Analyze one's behavior and the behavior of others in groups
  - Behave appropriately in a variety of social settings and under different circumstances
  - Work under the pressures of time and the work setting

- **Critical Thinking Skills**
  - Identify quickly and accurately the salient issues when making a decision or solving a problem
  - Identify a general principle to explain related experiences or data
  - Define the parameters of a problem
  - Identify reasonable criteria to assess the value or appropriateness of action or behavior
  - Adapt one's concepts and behavior to changing conventions and norms
  - Apply appropriate criteria to strategies and plans of action
  - Take a given premise or reason to its conclusion
  - Create innovative solutions to complex problems
  - Analyze from several perspectives the relationships among events and ideas
- **Management and Administrative Skills**
  - Analyze tasks
  - Identify people who can contribute to the task or solution of a problem
  - Identify resource materials useful to the finding of a solution
  - Delegate responsibility to complete a task
  - Motivate and lead others
  - Organize people and tasks to achieve specific goals

- **Value Setting Skills**
  - o Assess a course of action in terms of its long-range effects on general human welfare
  - o Make decisions that increase both the individual and common good
  - o Understand the contributions of the arts, literature, science, and technology
  - o Identify one's own value
  - o Assess one's own values in the face of difficult decisions

- **Personal Skills**
  - Analyze and learn from one's experience and the experience of others
  - Relate the skills learned in one place to the requirements of another
  - Match knowledge of one's own characteristics and abilities with information about an employment position or career opportunity
  - Identify, describe, and assess the relative importance of one's own needs
  - Develop personal goals and motivation
  - Identify and describe skills acquired from formal education and experience
  - Identify one's strengths and weaknesses. Accept and learn from criticism
  - Persist in the face of possible failure; let go of a project that cannot be carried out or does not merit the time and effort required to complete it
  - Earn the trust and confidence of others
  - Take risks
  - Accept responsibility and the consequences of one's actions
  - Present ones self effectively

Source: Breen, Paul and Urban Whitaker, San Francisco State University. 1975.

CHARTS AND TABLES

TABLE 15: EDUCATION PAYS

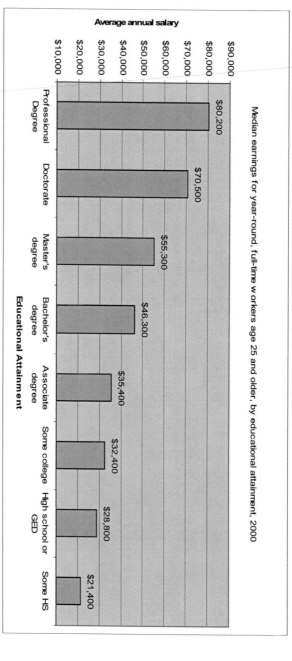

Median earnings for year-round, full-time workers age 25 and older, by educational attainment, 2000

Average annual salary

$90,000
$80,000
$70,000
$60,000
$50,000
$40,000
$30,000
$20,000
$10,000

Professional Degree — $80,200
Doctorate — $70,500
Master's degree — $55,300
Bachelor's degree — $46,300
Associate degree — $35,400
Some college — $32,400
High school or GED — $28,800
Some HS — $21,400

Educational Attainment

Source: U.S. Department of Labor, Bureau of Labor Statistics. 2000.

TABLE 16: SALARY SURVEY

Robert Half Technology – 2004 Salary Guide
Applications Development

Title	2003		2004		% chg
Systems Analyst	62,250	87,750	61,000	84,750	-2.8
Programmer/ Analyst	51,500	80,500	50,750	80,250	-0.8
Applications Architect	72,000	102,250	73,250	104,250	1.9
Business Systems Analyst	55,250	80,000	54,750	79,250	-0.9
Data/Database Administration					
Database Developer	67,750	100,500	65,250	98,000	-3.0
Database Administrator	69,750	101,750	67,000	97,750	-3.9
Database Analyst	59,000	80,000	58,250	79,750	-0.7
Data Modeler	66,500	88,250	66,500	88,750	0.3
Internet & E-Commerce					
Internet/Intranet Developer	51,250	73,750	51,000	72,500	-1.2
Internet/Intranet Administrator	53,500	75,250	49,250	71,250	-6.4
E-Mail/Groupware Administrator	46,750	67,000	47,250	66,750	0.2
Networking/Telecommunications					
Network Engineer	61,500	88,000	60,750	86,500	-1.5
LAN Administrator	45,500	65,750	43,750	62,500	-4.5
LAN/WAN Administrator	47,500	66,250	46,750	67,500	0.4
Telecommunications Specialist	49,500	71,750	47,000	67,000	-6.0
Security					

Data Security Analyst	65,500	89,000	67,000	90,750	2.1
Systems Security Administrator	65,000	91,750	66,000	91,500	0.5
Network Security Administrator	62,500	88,250	62,750	88,000	0.0
Software Development					
Software Engineer	64,250	97,000	62,500	94,750	-2.5
Developer	55,000	87,750	54,250	88,750	0.2
Technical Services Help Desk & Technical Support					
Desktop Support Analyst	51,000	67,250	47,000	65,000	-5.3
Systems Administrator	49,000	70,250	47,750	69,000	-2.1
Help Desk Tier 1	27,500	39,000	26,500	37,250	-4.1
Help Desk Tier 2	33,750	43,000	32,000	42,000	-3.6
Help Desk Tier 3	42,500	56,500	41,250	52,750	-5.1
Technical Writer	43,500	64,500	42,750	64,250	-0.9
Instructor/Trainer	43,500	65,750	43,750	62,250	-3.0
PC Technician	29,750	43,250	28,500	41,500	-4.1
Mainframe Systems Programmer	53,250	68,750	51,000	67,250	-3.1
Disaster Recovery Specialist	57,500	88,750	59,000	89,000	1.2

Source: "2004 Salary Guide" Robert Half Technology ® A *Robert Half International Company.* Menlo Park, California 2003.

CHART 1: EDUCATIONAL LEVEL [26]

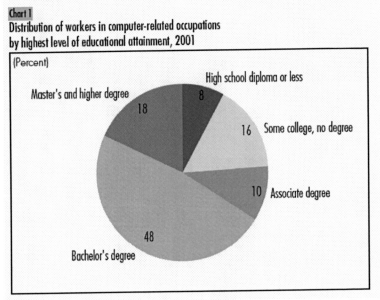

Chart 1
Distribution of workers in computer-related occupations
by highest level of educational attainment, 2001

Source: Moncarz, Roger "Training for Techies: Career preparation in information technology, *U.S. Department of Labor, Bureau of Labor Statistics*, fall 2002.

CHART 2: SOFT SKILLS

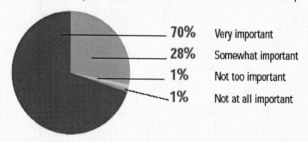

CIOs were asked, "When evaluating job candidates for information technology positions, how important are the individuals' 'soft' skills?" Their responses:

70% Very important
28% Somewhat important
1% Not too important
1% Not at all important

Source: Robert Half Technology survey of 1,400 CIOs from U.S. companies with more than 100 employees

Source: "2004 Salary Guide" Robert Half Technology ® A *Robert Half International Company*. Menlo Park, California 2003.

CHART 3: FASTEST GROWING SECTORS

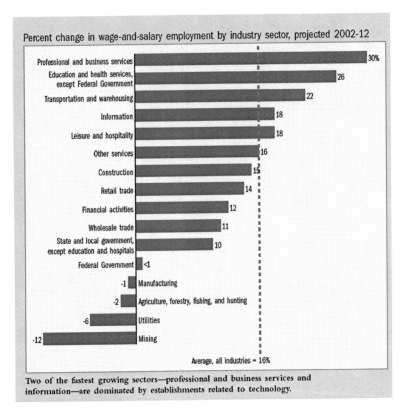

Percent change in wage-and-salary employment by industry sector, projected 2002-12

Sector	Percent
Professional and business services	30%
Education and health services, except Federal Government	26
Transportation and warehousing	22
Information	18
Leisure and hospitality	18
Other services	16
Construction	15
Retail trade	14
Financial activities	12
Wholesale trade	11
State and local government, except education and hospitals	10
Federal Government	<1
Manufacturing	-1
Agriculture, forestry, fishing, and hunting	-2
Utilities	-6
Mining	-12

Average, all industries = 16%

Two of the fastest growing sectors—professional and business services and information—are dominated by establishments related to technology.

Source: U.S. Department of Labor, Bureau of Labor Statistics. 2004.

ABOUT THE AUTHOR

Mr. Fisher started his career in IT in 1984 working for Citibank N.A. and U.S. Trust Company in New York City. He started his career as a Data Communications Technician. Upon completion of his Masters degree in Telecommunications from New York University, Mr. Fisher began his second career as a Technical Instructor/Trainer. As a consultant Mr. Fisher provided technical training to some of the largest Fortune 500 companies in the NYC Tri-State Area: New York University, Lederle Laboratories, Chase Manhattan Bank, The New School, Baruch College, Memorial Sloan Kettering to name a few. From Instructor/Trainer Mr. Fisher advanced into management positions in technical training.

In 1989 Mr. Fisher became the Director of Management & Information Technology Institutes at Long Island University. Prior to leaving New York Mr. Fisher completed a major curriculum development assignment for the State University of New York, Educational Opportunity Center.

In 1997 he relocated to Northern California where he has continued his career in the technology training area. Mr. Fisher has managed technology training programs for San Francisco State University, City and County of San Francisco, Bay Area Technology Education Collaborative, and the Oakland Unified School District. In addition to Mr. Fisher's consulting work, he teaches part-time at City College of San Francisco. An accomplished public speaker on Information Technology careers, Mr. Fisher has delivered seminars to a wide range of organizations such as:

- Long Island University
- San Francisco State University
- Street Tech, San Pablo, CA
- Cypress Technology Center, Oakland, CA
- James Irvine Conference Center, Oakland, CA
- State of California, Employment Development Department
- Oakland Public Library

Mr. Fisher is a consultant in the area of Information Technology training. His expertise covers is in: training, instructional design, curriculum development, adult learning theory, training program development, marketing, and management.

He can be reached at:
Ian K. Fisher
P.O. box 10562
Oakland, CA 94610
(866) 877-9791 phone/fax
ikfisher@onebox.com

COMMENTS? I welcome comments, corrections, and suggestions for improvement.

ORDERING INFORMATION

Mail check or money order (payable to Ian K. Fisher, in the amount of $19.95 plus shipping and taxes if applicable) to:
Ian K. Fisher
P.O. Box 10562
Oakland, CA 94610
**Questions?: call (866) 877-9791 or email
ikfisher@onebox.com
Fax: (866) 877-9791**

30-day money back Guarantee:
If you are not completely satisfied for any reason, you may return any item for a full refund, no questions asked.
Select Product:
❑ Book ($19.95)   ❑ Cassette ($10.95) ❑ CD/PDF ($10.95)

Name: _____

Address: _____

City: _____

State: _____Zip code:_____

Telephone: _____

Sales tax: Please add 7.75% for products shipped to California addresses.
Shipping by air: U.S. only: $4.00 for first book, cassette, or CD; $2.00 for each additional product.

Please send me more information on:
❑ Speaking/seminars   ❑ Consulting   ❑ Training

CREDIT CARD ORDERS NOT ACCEPTED

B IBLIOGRAPHY

1 Baker, Stephen and Manjeet Kripalani "Programming jobs are heading overseas by the thousands. Is there any way for the U.S. to stay on top?" *BusinessWeek Online*, March 1, 2004.

2 Safer, Morley "Out of India", aired on *CBS 60-Minutes News Magazine*, August 1, 2004.

3 Field, Tom "Outsourcing 10 Years That Shook IT" *CIO Magazine*, October 1, 1999.

4 Koch, Christopher "Special Report Off-shore Outsourcing: The Politics" *CIO Magazine*, September 1, 2003.

5 Field, Tom "Outsourcing 10 Years That Shook IT" *CIO Magazine*, October 1, 1999.

6 Safer, Morley "Out of India", aired on *CBS 60-Minutes News Magazine*, August 1, 2004.

7 McCue, Andy and Ed Frauenhei "Bangalore may be gaining on Silicon Valley" *San Francisco Chronicle*, July 29, 2004

8 Bolles, Richard Nelson "The 1994 What Color is Your Parachute – a Practical Manual for Job hunters & Career-Changers". *Ten Speed Press* 1994. Page 163.

9 Bolles, Richard Nelson "The 1994 What Color is Your Parachute – a Practical Manual for Job hunters & Career-Changers". *Ten Speed Press* 1994. Page 166.

[10] Moncarz, Roger "Training for Techies: Career preparation in information technology". *U.S. Department of Labor, Bureau of Labor Statistics*, fall 2002.

[11] Bartlett, Kenneth "The Perceived Influence of Industry-Sponsored Credentials". University of Minnesota, Copyright 2002. Reprinted with permission: *National Research Center for Career and Technical Education, University of Minnesota, St. Paul, MN*, The National Dissemination Center for Career and Technical Education, Ohio State University, Columbus, OH.

[12] *The Association of College and Research Libraries* "Information Literacy Competency Standards for Higher Education" a *Division of the American Library Association*, January 8, 2000.

[13] Moncarz, Roger "Training for Techies: Career preparation in information technology". *U.S. Department of Labor, Bureau of Labor Statistics*, fall 2002.

[14] Moncarz, Roger "Training for Techies: Career preparation in information technology". *U.S. Department of Labor, Bureau of Labor Statistics*, fall 2002.

[15] The Joint Task Force for Computing Curricula "Computing Curricula 2004 Overview Report – A Guide to Undergraduate Degree Programs in Computing" A cooperative project of: *The Association for Computing Machinery (ACM), The Association for Information Systems (AIS), The Computer Society (IEEE-CS)*. Strawman Draft June 1, 2004.

[16] Moncarz, Roger "Training for Techies: Career preparation in information technology". *U.S. Department of Labor, Bureau of Labor Statistics*, fall 2002.

[17] Immerwahr, John and Tony Foleno "Great Expectations How the Public and Parents – White, African-American, and Hispanic – View Higher Education" *Public Agenda*, May 2000.

[18] Bolles, Richard Nelson "The Three Boxes of Life", *Ten Speed Press* 1981. Page 138.

[19] Bolles, Richard Nelson "What Color is your Parachute? 2004 Edition A Practical Manual for Job-Hunters & Career Changers", *Ten Speed Press* 2004. Page 42.

[20] Bolles, Richard Nelson "What Color is your Parachute? 2004 Edition A Practical Manual for Job-Hunters & Career Changers", *Ten Speed Press* 2004. Page 45.

[21] Beatty, Richard H. "The Resume Kit" third edition. Published by *John Wiley Sons Inc.* 1995.

[22] Beatty, Richard H. "The Perfect Cover Letter". Published by John Wiley & Sons, Inc. 1989.

[23] *U.S. Department of Labor, Bureau of Labor Statistics*, Bulletin 2540, Occupational Outlook Handbook. Date: February 27, 2004

[24] Bartlett, Kenneth "The Perceived Influence of Industry-Sponsored Credentials". University of Minnesota, Copyright 2002. Reprinted with permission: *National Research Center for Career and Technical Education, University of Minnesota, St. Paul, MN*, The National Dissemination Center for Career and Technical Education, Ohio State University, Columbus, OH.

[25]Bartlett, Kenneth "The Perceived Influence of Industry-Sponsored Credentials". University of Minnesota, Copyright 2002. Reprinted with permission: *National Research Center for Career and Technical Education, University of Minnesota, St. Paul, MN*, The National Dissemination Center for Career and Technical Education, Ohio State University, Columbus, OH.

[26] Moncarz, Roger "Training for Techies: Career preparation in information technology". *U.S. Department of Labor, Bureau of Labor Statistics*, fall 2002.